RECLAIMING
FAITH

MICHAEL COREN

RECLAIMING
FAITH

Inclusion, Grace, and Tolerance

Cormorant Books

The publisher gratefully acknowledges the support of the Canada Council for the Arts and the Ontario Arts Council for its publishing program. We acknowledge the financial support of the Government of Canada through the Canada Book Fund (CBF) for our publishing activities, and the Government of Ontario through Ontario Creates, an agency of the Ontario Ministry of Culture, and the Ontario Book Publishing Tax Credit Program.

LIBRARY AND ARCHIVES CANADA CATALOGUING IN PUBLICATION

Title: Reclaiming faith / Michael Coren.
Names: Coren, Michael, author.
Identifiers: Canadiana (print) 20190149183 | Canadiana (ebook) 20190149205 | ISBN 9781770865648 (softcover) | ISBN 9781770865655 (html)
Subjects: LCSH: Jesus Christ—Example. | LCSH: Jesus Christ—Teachings. | LCSH: Jesus Christ—Political and social views. | LCSH: Christian life—Biblical teaching. | LCSH: Christian life. | LCSH: Christianity.
Classification: LCC BT304.2 .C67 2019 | DDC 232.9/04—dc23

Cover design: angeljohnguerra.com
Interior text design: Tannice Goddard, tannicegdesigns.ca
Printer: Houghton Boston

Printed and bound in Canada.

CORMORANT BOOKS INC.
260 SPADINA AVENUE, SUITE 502, TORONTO, ON, M5T 2E4
www.cormorantbooks.com

CONTENTS

INTRODUCTION

This is a collection of articles and columns from a number of magazines and newspapers from the past five years, all of them about faith. To be more specific, they are about *my* faith, which is Christianity. To be even more precise, a liberal and Catholic interpretation of Christianity which in my case has led me to the Anglican Church. The prism through which I view the world is a Christian one, based both on and in my relationship with Jesus Christ. That language may be jarring to the general reader but it is nevertheless true. Sometimes these columns are directly pertinent to what it means to be a Christian, sometimes I analyse various issues and challenges within the Church, sometimes comment on the secular world but from a Christian point of view.

Contrary to what some people think, there is an appetite for such work, as the responses to my columns have revealed over the years. Nor are these numerous responses only from Christians, but actually most from agnostics, doubters, and even quite militant atheists. Some of them are, of course, critical and even angry — and sometimes for good reasons — but most are curious, intrigued, and even supportive. I like to think that I am an informed writer, and on my better days I may even be intelligent, but whatever my failings and weaknesses, I am always honest. That seems to appeal to people, whatever their faith or lack thereof. I am not trying to convert people or to proselytize, at least not in a direct manner! If someone is encouraged by my writings to inquire further or to be strengthened in their faith (and I know that this has happened) I am delighted. In the world of the polemic and the sound bite, especially when it comes to matters of religion, perhaps I can break the rhythm a little. I certainly hope so.

I also approach the issues with a radical Gospel message, one that by its nature is progressive. I look neither left nor right but up, yet it cannot be denied that a faith that demands change cannot by definition be on the side of an unjust status quo. This is surprising to many readers, who have been beaten over the years into assuming that Christianity is right wing and even reactionary. I don't blame them at all for this and I'm even a small part of the problem. Until around six years ago — and this is something I cover in my columns so won't dwell on here — I was part of that conservative approach. The theme and recurring message of my work now, and one that I hope is reflected in this book, is that Christianity is a forward-looking, liberating, and even revolutionary belief system that obliges us to question power and authority and to dream new dreams, centred on justice, peace, kindness, and hope.

All of these pieces appeared in professional publications so were edited then, and the small amount of further editing that has taken place for this book is minimal — I believe that a writer's work should stand in its original form; it would somehow be unfair or cheating to change something with hindsight. Some of the themes are repeated and perhaps even some of the phrases, but this is inevitable. There are only so many ways to explain, for example, what the Bible says about LGBT+ people, or the way we should treat the poor or marginalized.

I would like to thank the editors at *Maclean's*, *The Walrus*, the

Toronto Star, The Globe and Mail, iPolitics, The United Church Observer, and CBC Opinion for publishing my writing and for having an interest in issues that matter so very much, but are too frequently neglected or rejected. They often improved my work, but I, of course, take full responsibility for everything written in this book. I also want to thank my teachers and colleagues at the Divinity School at Trinity College, University of Toronto, where I spent three years studying for a Master of Divinity, graduating in May 2019. The symbiotic relationship between the academic study of faith and religion and journalistic commentary on those issues is severely undervalued, and it's been a privilege and a pleasure to have a foot in both camps, as it were.

Thanks also to the Anglican Church of Canada and the Diocese of Niagara — while my words are entirely my own and I do not speak in any way or manner for the Church or the diocese, both places have become for me a free and safe venue for spiritual growth and evolution. To my friends in Canada and the U.K., you know who you are, I will be forever grateful and always devoted.

Jesus, Me, and the Way It Ought to Be

The Walrus, July 21, 2015

TEN YEARS AGO, in July 2005, the Canadian government made same-sex marriage the law of the land. Various provincial courts had recognized marriage equality, but now it had parliamentary weight and royal assent. There was no turning back. As with all good laws, Bill C-38, or the Civil Marriage Act, largely affirmed what most people already accepted as self-evident: that the rights and obligations of matrimony apply to two men or two women as much as they do to a man and woman.

It is only a matter of time before the United States as a whole follows Canada's example. Whereas a decade ago no viable Republican candidate could even flirt with supporting the idea, today we have Marco Rubio and Jeb Bush explaining that while they still oppose marriage equality, they nevertheless would attend a gay or lesbian wedding if someone they "cared for" were involved.

All of which is to say: a decade on and quite a bit has changed, including me.

This past February, a conservative Roman Catholic blog, Contra| Diction, gave me perhaps my best headline ever: "Michael Coren Complicit in Destruction of Souls Who Practice Homosexuality, Pt 1"

(I'm still waiting for part two). It was one of countless posts, tweets, and articles that have condemned me for coming out in favour of same-sex marriage. I've also been fired from columns that I wrote for years, been banned from various Catholic TV and radio stations, had speeches cancelled, and been accused of cheating on my wife. My children have been called gay, and I have been compared to a child molester and a murderer.

These are new experiences for me. Until last year, I was considered something of a champion of social conservatism in Canada and was well-known among politically active Christians. I hosted a nightly show on Crossroads Television for twelve years, was a syndicated *Sun* columnist, and wrote briskly selling books with such titles as *Why Catholics Are Right*. Today, as a decade of same-sex marriage waves its arms at Pride parades, I am working away at a new book, *Coming Out: A Christian's Change of Heart and Mind Over Gay Marriage*. Oh, dear. How and why did it go so terribly wrong?

I grew up in an intensely secular home in England. Three of my grandparents were Jewish, but my mother's mother — and it's the maternal line that has to be kosher — was not. This was the 1960s and '70s, and homosexuality always was mentioned in whispers. When people like my parents used the word queer, it was less pejorative than descriptive. The only acceptable face of it was on TV — British comics camping it up and playing effeminate stereotypes, all the while assuring us that in real life they could barely keep their pants on when attractive women walked past. They were, of course, all gay men off camera, but never the caricatures they created on TV. Oh, the irony.

From a working-class home, I was propelled into university and then into London literary society, where I first encountered, at least in its inchoate stages, a proud and openly gay community. My first book, released in 1984, came about with the help of a highly respected — and gay — theatre critic, Jim Hiley, who recommended me to a publisher.

There was no other way a twenty-five-year-old would have landed a contract. Then I went to work at the *New Statesman*, the country's premier left-leaning magazine, when Christopher Hitchens still was on the staff. Ours was a masthead full of privately educated, clever, good-looking boys — all seduced by socialism. Gay influence was everywhere we looked, but none of us dared speak its name.

In 1985, I joined the Roman Catholic Church, which employs more gay men than any other institution in the world — despite leading the culture war against gay rights. That's not to say the Church is full of hatred and homophobia, but it has, as with some elements of the Protestant right, elevated the issue to a level that has no basis in scripture. Jesus never mentions same-sex attraction. Lesbianism is not referred to at all in the Old Testament. The letters of the Apostles mention homosexuality only briefly.

What references do exist make up a tiny, insignificant sliver of theological texts, a splash of minutiae within Christian thought. But it has become the prism through which myriad conservative Christians, particularly Catholics, judge one's faith and conviction. It's tragic on many levels.

As a newly minted Catholic journalist, I was thrown into the marriage debate, and I wrote and broadcast about the issue many times, defending the doctrine I had adopted as my converted creed. The issue was never a major part of my work, but, goodness, it sometimes felt like it. And I'm sure to gays and lesbians, who were understandably more interested in my views on them than on the Middle East, taxation policies, or Quebec, I probably became something of a monster. I said some bloody careless things, and at the very least empowered those who genuinely did have a hateful agenda.

But I never hated, because I couldn't. I had too many gay friends, had been helped by too many gay people, simply did not care viscerally about the issue — which, in a way, makes my behaviour worse.

It's not that I was dishonest or disingenuous. More than anything, I was dogmatic.

Once I'd taken up the banner of anti–marriage equality, it became increasingly difficult to cast it off. I may sound weak, even pathetic and cowardly, but by 2012 I was hosting a daily show on the invincibly right-wing Sun News Network, writing columns for four Catholic publications, speaking to Catholic groups throughout North America and the United Kingdom, appearing on Catholic radio, and publishing Catholic books. A mingling of income, self-perception, and reputation made it difficult to say what I truly felt.

Finally, in 2013, Uganda's biting homophobia brought me to my senses. Canada's then foreign minister, John Baird, gently criticized a Kampala official about proposed legislation to further criminalize homosexuality — even to make it a capital offence. Baird, who had been a great defender of persecuted Christians, was stridently condemned by conservative Christian groups for criticizing noble Uganda and questioning its independence. I was outraged at Uganda and outraged at the treatment of Baird, and I said so on TV and in print.

And just like that, I realized how often the opposition to marriage equality was — and is — motivated not by a sense of duty to defend traditional wedlock, but by a profound dislike of gays and lesbians.

I was bombarded with accusatory comments and stunned by how an innocuous, fundamentally Christian response to persecution could provoke such malice. The more I was pushed, the more I felt that I needed to speak out. In April 2014, I decided to come clean, or at least have a good wash, in my weekly *Sun* column. "In the past six months I have been parachuted into clouds of new realization and empathy regarding gay issues, largely and ironically because of the angry and hateful responses of some people to my defence of persecuted gay men and women in Africa and Russia," I wrote. "This wasn't reasonable opposition but a tainted monomania with no understanding of humanity and an obsession with sex rather than love."

Then I went further: "I have evolved on this single subject because I can no longer hide behind comfortable banalities, have realized that love triumphs judgment, and know that the conversation between Christians and gays has to transform...I am sick and tired of defining the word of God by a single and not even particularly important subject."

I was careful in my column not to contradict Catholic theology and didn't even mention same-sex marriage. But that didn't prevent an overwhelmingly hostile reaction from the Christian right. The response from the LGBT+ community, however, was quite different. I had come rather late to the secular dance (if fairly early to the Christian one) around this subject, but gay men and women from all over the world sent me kind notes and emails. I can't imagine a *Sun* column was ever so widely read in gay circles, and it was impossible not to juxtapose the two reactions: anger and abuse from one group, forgiveness and gratitude from the other.

As a middle-aged, very white, very straight, very Christian man, I was obliged, first reluctantly and then eagerly, to explore the complex dynamic between faith and homosexuality and to work out a new narrative. The crux of that narrative: God is love. The love I felt when I first saw my newborn children, when I watched my mother dissolve into Alzheimer's, when I found my late father's diaries that spoke of his pride in our family, when I feel closest to the Christ I worship. Jesus spoke of love for everybody and called for forgiveness, justice, truth, turning the other cheek.

As my faith has deepened over the years, I have tried to broaden the circle of inclusive love rather than guard the borders of what I once thought was Christian truth. Instead of holding the door firm, I want to hold it wide open. I have realized that Christianity is a permanent revolution, a state of being in which we believers must challenge our preconceptions every moment of every day. How dare I — with all of my brokenness and sordid, banal sinfulness — criticize someone simply because he or she wants to live life fully? How the hell dare I?

The standard Christian response to homosexuality is the familiar but entirely inadequate mantra "love the sinner but hate the sin." In other words, a gay person's sexual and romantic attraction — much of their being and personality, and all that they want in a lasting relationship — is sinful, but they themselves are just fine. By way of analogy, the teachings go, Christians love alcoholics but not alcoholism, love those who commit adultery but not the act of adultery itself. Such logic presupposes that same-sex attraction is no more central to a person's identity than substance abuse or unfaithfulness — which any reasonable person knows to be untrue.

More extreme Christians believe that one can pray away the gay and that gay people can be changed, which is why some continue to support so-called conversion therapy. They bristle at the suggestion that gays and lesbians are born that way: that thread of biological reasoning implies God created people who are powerfully disposed toward sinful lifestyles, which seems dubious no matter your religious tendencies.

The whole thing is like some theological rabbit hole that gets darker as you descend. It's also dishonest. I have spoken to hundreds of Catholic groups and parishes over the years, and I would estimate that one out of every three priests is gay, and by no means are they all celibate. (Others have put the number as high as fifty percent.) The joke at the Vatican is that if the Swiss Guard find a priest in bed with a man, they are to ignore it. If with a woman, report it at once. There's humour in that joke, but also horrifying hypocrisy.

There are Catholic priests in Canada living with their partners, and some of these men are prominent clerics. Living that lie, existing in such a state of moral dissonance, is achingly damaging. One former priest told me that he once visited a senior bishop (I am being purposely vague here) to explain that he was gay and needed to leave the priesthood. The bishop responded that it was okay to stay in the Church and that the priest could have a parish outside of the city, where he could live with his lover. None of this, believe me, is shocking to those who truly know the Church as insiders.

Evangelical denominations have far less of a subtly embedded gay culture (in part because they permit their male clerics to marry women), but there are infamous cases of high-profile Protestant critics of homosexuality being outed. Their hypocrisy takes another form: most evangelical churches blithely will remarry divorced people (even ministers can be divorced), despite the fact that Jesus, who doesn't say a single word about homosexuality, is fiercely critical of dissolving a marriage. Indeed, in the Roman, Greek, and Jewish cultures in which he lived — where divorce was common and easy — his stance was revolutionary. Yet his followers have ignored those Christian teachings while inventing others on sexuality.

When it comes to same-sex marriage, history is not on the side of conservatives. Academics, popular historians, and theologians alike are re-exploring the context of Biblical passages and coming to a new understanding of what scripture says about homosexuality (a term not invented until the nineteenth century).

Sodom has much for which to answer. But even the Genesis story of Sodom and Gomorrah is more about hospitality — protecting one's guests and neighbours, and loving God rather than oneself — than about condemning gays and lesbians. Remember, Lot offers the rape mob outside his house his virgin daughters instead of the male angels who happen to be visiting. Not exactly family values. The anti-gay interpretation is an anachronistic, tendentious one. When the Old Testament speaks of homosexuality elsewhere, it lists it alongside unacceptable combinations of cloth, eating the wrong foods, having sex with a woman when she is menstruating, and so on. If we're to accept the modern applicability of these sins, we're pretty much all of us irredeemable sinners. If we pick and choose what's still a sin, we're hypocrites.

We should read the apostle Paul's rejection of homosexuality in his letter to the Romans in a similar spirit. Paul chooses the word exchange, which implies straight men who use boys, usually young teenagers, for loveless sex. This was common in Greek and Roman cultures, and Paul condemns abusive power dynamics with catamites as selfish.

A magazine is not the place to discuss the finer points of theology (I'll save that for the book). But what I can say here, with complete confidence, is that too many Christians convince themselves that there are no questions to be asked, only answers to be recited. Ironically, because most young people in the West can't even comprehend opposition to same-sex marriage and full equality, and because such acceptance will inexorably increase and spread throughout the world, we may see a time when the only opposition to what is loving and fair will come from an institution that regards itself as an icon of love and fairness. This contradiction will make it impossible to preach the gospel. Christians will be defined by their obstinate clinging to an outdated antipathy.

Recently, I had lunch in downtown Toronto with the publisher of a leading gay Internet site. We talked shop, laughed, drank wine. Family came up, and I showed him some photographs of my wife — the one I am supposed to have cheated on — and he remarked on her good looks. There was a long pause. He turned his phone around and showed me a picture of his husband. Then he looked up: "I was hesitant to show that to you. I was uncomfortable with how you might react." I felt ashamed and very small.

"You know," he continued, "you had quite an effect on my life. I'd just come to Toronto — wasn't even out yet — and I was meeting with a colleague. He went off to the washroom, and I read the newspaper he had with him. It was the *Toronto Sun*, and you had a column in it that was critical of gay people. Of me, really. It broke my heart."

The two of us are friends now. But, good Lord, I still have some apologizing to do. Quite a lot, in fact.

CHURCH AND STATE
AND STATE OF CHURCH

Maclean's, May 8, 2019

UNTIL THE RECENT massacre of Christians in Sri Lanka, it's likely that most people in North America and Europe considered the idea of the persecution of Christians as little more than conservative hyperbole, a cry of wolf to defend those with reactionary views regarding equal marriage or abortion. In fact, those false claims from western Christians and their friends have done enormous harm, because the truth is that Christians are certainly persecuted in large parts of Asia, Africa, and the Middle East, to a shocking and hideous degree. I've been writing and broadcasting about this issue for more than two decades and the problem has, if anything, become even worse.

A recent report commissioned by the U.K. government concluded: "The inconvenient truth is that the overwhelming majority (80%) of persecuted religious believers are Christians," and that "forms of persecution ranging from routine discrimination in education, employment and social life up to genocidal attacks against Christian communities have led to a significant exodus of Christian believers." Commenting on the report, British Foreign Secretary Jeremy Hunt stated, "What we have forgotten in this atmosphere of political correctness is actually the Christians that are being persecuted are some of the poorest people on the planet. In the Middle East, the population of Christians used to be about twenty percent; now it's five percent."

Father Nadim Nassar is a Syrian born to a Christian family in Latakia. He studied in Lebanon, and now lives in London where he is director of the Awareness Foundation, an ecumenical charity working in Europe, North America, the Middle East, and Hong Kong to encourage diversity, acceptance, and peace. He is also an Anglican priest, the Church of England's only Syrian clergyman. His latest book is *The Culture of God* (Hodder and Stoughton) and he is in Toronto to receive an honorary doctorate from the prestigious Trinity School of Divinity at the University of Toronto.

Were you surprised by what happened in Sri Lanka?

No, not at all, and the ignorance in the West of what is going on has annoyed me for decades. It seems that the more media we have, the more ignorant we have become. America declares that ISIS is defeated in Syria and Iraq. Total nonsense. ISIS is well, alive and kicking, in the form of an ideology. And if you think ideology can be defeated by a bullet you are mistaken. The ISIS ideology has been exported and nowhere is safe. I don't want to sound polemical, but this is the truth. It's not just Islam of course. Religious extremism is a virus that may have begun in the near east with Islam, but has now spread internationally to mosque, temple, church, everywhere. The Christian right in the United States, Hindu nationalism in India, and so on.

Yet in your country of Syria, and in Iraq, Palestine, and Jordan, Christians historically enjoyed a certain equality and even respect.

Yes, but there is a reason for that. No Christian would dream, for example, to be the President of Iraq or Syria. We were harmless, we weren't seen as a threat. There were some exceptions. For example, we had a Christian Prime Minister once in Syria, one of the founders of the UN, but this was never taught to us at school. It was written out of our history. Christians also played a major role in pan-Arabism, or Arab nationalism, as long ago as the early twentieth century, but part of this was because the Arab identity was always seen as less dangerous than the Muslim identity — Arabism might include us, political Islam never would. We have always been between a rock and a hard place, but it was never as difficult and dangerous as it is now.

How did the Iraq War and western intervention in Syria influence the situation for Christians?

It made it much worse. No doubt. Arab Muslims see us as an extension of the west in the region, but in the west we're invisible. Fanaticism was empowered by the chaos, and Christians suffered accordingly. Westerners might know of the road to Damascus and St. Paul, but they think of Damascus as some imaginary place, like Camelot, rather a city in my country. There are people who think that the west intervened to help Christians. Rubbish! They intervened to extend their own interests.

When I first came to Europe thirty years ago people would ask me when I became a Christian. Our faith pre-dates Islam, pre-dates Christianity in Europe and North America. Look, the entire situation is a stain on the world and it's shameful how we have done so little to prevent such suffering and tragedy. A million dead in my country and so many more in Iraq. Twelve million people moving from place to place, frightened and in such terrible need. Within all of this is the plight of Christians, always under threat.

Do you think a fear of being labelled as Islamophobic has prevented people from speaking up about the Islamist persecution of Christians?

Yes, for sure. We have created no-go areas when it comes to comment. I don't like to use the word "Islamophobia." I am from the near east, I know Islam, most of my friends are Muslim, and the idea that I have an issue with them is ridiculous. I shouldn't even have to say this. Yes, there is suspicion and even hatred of Muslims in the West, yes there is. But we need to be honest, we can't be frightened of discussing certain issues. Muslim leaders point to ISIS and the jihadists and say, "These people aren't Muslims." No, that won't do. Because those they condemn then turn around and say, "No, we're the real Muslims, you're not." Muslim leadership has to deal with the fanatics, the killers, and the first step is to admit the truth. They are Muslims, and now deal with this problem.

But I also reject the term "persecuted Christians." Yes, we are persecuted. But don't think us as people are to be pitied, to be put aside as a group to feel sorry for and then forget. We have played an enormous role in Arab society, we still do. Work with us, as partners and not some victim group. We're persecuted, but don't simply label us and then conveniently reject us as victims.

Do you have hope or does the situation seem beyond repair?

I'm a Christian, I have to have hope, and I do. But if we take North Africa as a precedent it's very discouraging. Tunisia, Algeria, Morocco — no Christians. That's because the colonizers, the French, were brutal and once they withdrew so did Christianity. The French killed Christianity in North Africa. The issue now is that the bond of trust has been broken between Muslims and Christians in the region. When I return to Syria I wear my clerical collar, but I'm careful, members of my family who live there don't wear crucifixes outside of their shirts. And this is now, with the war allegedly over and in areas that are supposed to be safe. Yes, the near east could become like North Africa, of course it could. All I can do is to try to make people aware, to never let go, never stop, and, as you asked me, to have hope.

ISRAEL FOLAU IS one of the best, most highly paid, and famous rugby footballers in the world. He's played more than sixty times for his country, is the fourth highest scoring Australian international player of all time, and even has a street named after him. He's also a Pentecostal Christian who has gotten into trouble in the past for his public anti-gay statements, and has now posted on Instagram that "drunks, homosexuals, adulterers, liars, fornicators, thieves, atheists and idolaters" are going to hell.

This was the last straw for Rugby Australia, the sport's governing authority, who have terminated his contract for what they describe as a "high level" breach of the players' code of conduct. This comes as Australia prepares for the rugby World Cup later this year. It's been confirmed that Folau, a superstar who would make any national team, will not be selected.

The chief executive of Rugby Australia, Raelene Castle, has explained that there had been earlier warnings, and apparent agreements from the player that had then been broken. She insisted, "This is not a religious discussion, this is a discussion around the employee-employer relationship." Folau has been condemned by many in the rugby community, but England player Billy Vunipola, also an evangelical, has been severely reprimanded for publicly supporting Folau and posting that, "Man was made for woman to pro create that was the goal no?"

It doesn't take a genius to realize that adulterers, liars, and fornicators aren't the people who are at issue here. Atheists are, but most particularly — and dangerously — is the LGBT+ community. Nor is this some academic or morally and politically neutral issue, because there are still seventy countries where homosexuality is illegal, and seven of them impose the death penalty for consensual same-sex acts. In two dozen other states gay relationships can lead to arrest and imprisonment. Just recently Brunei introduced new laws punishing gay sex with death by stoning.

As a Christian, I find Folau's post to be painfully reductive, theologically flimsy, and totally contrary to the unconditional love not suggested, but demanded by Jesus. It pains me that a teaching so pristine in its gentleness and so affirming of the human condition should be twisted into a creed of loathing. Be that as it may, however, does this man have a right to say these things, and should he be penalized for so doing?

They are two different questions, of course. In a perfect world hideous statements like this would not be made, but both the law and our cultural and philosophical assumptions about free speech are designed precisely to respond to imperfection. People do offend and will offend, and beyond libel and direct calls for violence, most of us would allow the sewers to breathe. Partly because we can't completely prevent it, but also because any attempt to over-police free speech would have deeply troubling and even authoritarian consequences.

The other aspect of this is whether such undoubtedly noxious comments should enjoy a special protection because they are made under the guise of religiosity. When, for example, in 2017 Kevin Pillar called Jason Motte a "faggot" he made a long and seemingly heartfelt apology and accepted his two-game suspension. It was a barroom slur, made in anger, and while unacceptable had none of the horribly eschatological underpinnings involved in the Israel Folau posting. The Australian has made similar comments in the past and gone unpunished, and even now there are many Christians and libertarians rushing to his defence. He himself is aggressively unrepentant.

It seems to me that the response to this latest situation is about right. The man does have a right, has to have a right, to believe and even proclaim that most of the world's population is destined for hell, but similarly he has no special privilege to make such hideous predictions without reaction. Most of those who pay to watch him play, or buy the products he endorses, disagree with him, and many are members of the litany he claims will suffer for eternity. It is outrageous to insist that they remain passive in all this. There's something else. Athletes who represent their country do exactly that — represent. There are many athletes whose religious beliefs are not of the mainstream, but they appreciate the need to separate what is their right to believe from what is their responsibility not to alienate and marginalize.

While Folau will now be lionized by the Christian right, along with the league of people who have refused to bake cakes, make dresses, or take photographs for same-sex weddings, his story is actually a tragic one. His sporting gifts will not be seen by the millions who used to watch him, and the faith he claims to embrace so deeply will once again be tarnished.

Perhaps the last and best word should go to the former captain of the Welsh rugby team, Gareth Thomas, who came out in 2009. "Telling teammates I was gay was the toughest thing I've ever done," he said. His coach said to him, "You can't go through it alone, and these people love you." Love. Sounds just a little more Christ-like than what poor, misled Israel Folau has been saying.

iPolitics, April 23, 2019

THE MASS MURDER of Christians in Sri Lanka stunned many observers, not only because of the obvious barbarism of the act, but because the prime target was Christians, and during Easter and in church. For those of us who have been writing and broadcasting for decades about the persecution of Christians, however, this obscenity came as little surprise.

Back in 2012, I was hosting a nightly television show and on one occasion my guest was a Christian minister from the Middle East. He asked me if he could put a Bible on the desk in front of him during the interview. I politely told him that I'd rather he didn't, because it might look like proselytizing. He replied that he understood, but that this particular Bible might be of interest to the viewers. It had been in Our Lady of Salvation Syriac Catholic cathedral in Baghdad on October 31, 2010, when a Sunni Muslim terrorist group known as the Islamic State of Iraq attacked the church, murdering fifty-eight people and wounding more than seventy-five.

The book being held in front of me was almost beyond reading, as its pages were glued together in purple lumps, sticky with the blood of the men, women and children who had been slaughtered that warm evening in a place of peace, in a city where Christians had lived and flourished for almost 2,000 years. This was not a holy book to be preached from, but a holy book of martyrdom that preached. Its hardly legible pages spoke entire volumes, its red-turned-to-brown stains cried out to a still largely indifferent world.

The Baghdad attack, however, was merely one example of the war on Christianity. Even Pope Francis, hardly militant in these areas, told a group of forty Jewish leaders, including the then head of the World Jewish Congress, Ronald S. Lauder, "First it was your turn and now it is our turn." In February 2014, U.S. representative Chris Smith, chairman of the congressional panel that oversees international human rights issues, told a congressional subcommittee that discussion of "anti-Christian persecution is not meant to minimize the suffering of other religious minorities who are imprisoned or killed for their beliefs," but to make it clear that Christians "remain the most persecuted religious group the world over."

More than 300 million Christians are threatened with violence or face legal discrimination, forced conversion, and daily threats. In countries such as Egypt, Saudi Arabia, Pakistan, Nigeria, and elsewhere they are frequently imprisoned and tortured on false charges of drinking and blasphemy, and in Iraq the exodus of Christians has been so great that the faith may even cease to exist in any meaningful sense in years to come.

But this is a good example of why we have to be very selective and informed in how and what we judge. Saddam Hussein was a brute, but he didn't persecute Christians. It was the western invasion of Iraq that smashed the stability of the place, empowering Islamist groups and leading to the full-scale attack on the Christian minority. Similarly in Syria, Christians are generally protected, and in Palestine the national conversation was traditionally shaped by Greek Orthodox Christians.

In Egypt the story is sadly different; in Turkey there is hardly even a concept of a "Turkish Christian"; and in Pakistan the once respected Christian minority is now intimidated and frightened.

This is not an issue of Islam refusing to accept Christianity, but of radicalized Islam and of ignorant, sadistic fanatics not accepting anybody but their own — they also slaughter Muslims who refuse to adopt their gruesome twisting of the Muslim faith. Yet Christians are without doubt the main victims of this systemic persecution and violence, and the western world says relatively little.

The reasons are complex, but one of the causes is that conservative Christians in North America and Europe so frequently claim victimhood, usually when they show intolerance towards LGBT+ people. This absurd boast of martyrdom leads to cynicism about the very real horrors experienced by Christians in other parts of the world. On a grander scale, when George W. Bush launched imperial campaigns in majority-Muslim areas and spoke of a Christian motive there was an understandable, if misplaced, anger. If Bush and his people were Christian, how could Christians be vulnerable and persecuted?

Then there is sheer ignorance, with the political and media class having so little experience of peoples outside of their comfort zone. There's an assumption that Christians are somehow like them, are white and secure, powerful and prosperous, and thus not the correct demographic at all for sympathy. The middle-class solipsism of all this is nauseating.

The inescapable fact is that Christians are indeed a highly persecuted group in large parts of the world, and that Christianity even faces disappearance in the places where it was born. It is not a western faith, but one rooted deeply in the Middle East, and its adherents in much of that region, and in Asia and Africa, demand our help and solidarity. If we choose between marginalized groups, and ignore one for whatever reason we conjure, we are failing in our intelligence, compassion, and humanity.

The Globe and Mail, March 29, 2018

FOR MUCH OF its four decades on the air, *100 Huntley Street* was a familiar address on the Canadian TV dial — a place where many people seeking a break from the cares of the world could feel they'd found a refuge. The show was founded by the late David Mainse, whom I knew well, and who, over the quarter-century that he hosted the show, made viewers feel welcome in one of the country's most hospitable living rooms.

Although a product of a traditional Pentecostal background, David was a kind, tolerant, and forward-looking man. I remember him calling me in Britain in 2001, when my father died. He didn't want to preach, only to tell me he was there for me. That combination of simple kindness, unalloyed by sermonizing, was typical of David's Christianity, and under his guidance, *100 Huntley Street* was far less political, less angrily conservative than its American TV counterparts. I was not the only one who thought so. Tony Campolo, a leader of the American evangelical left, once put it this way to me: "In the United States, every Christian television door was closed to me. But when I came to Canada, everyone at *Huntley* called me right away."

That open-door policy was not to last. I had been a regular guest host of *Huntley* when, in 2015, I publicly endorsed equal marriage. Soon after, an email arrived from the show's producers. "It is felt that with the high public profile you have in relation to gay marriage ... we have to part our ways." I responded that I'd never mentioned the topic on their show, and would never do so, out of respect for what I knew was their position on sexuality. The response: "People know what you think."

In fact, had viewers known the full extent of my thinking, they would have had even greater cause for concern — concern about their community's own survival. For I am convinced, as are many believers, that Christianity is challenged as never before.

But the challenge comes not from popular hostility — no matter how much Christians might see themselves as a persecuted minority. No, to my mind, the threat facing the Church is the very real prospect of public irrelevance. So many Canadians have turned away from Christianity. And yet, they are longing to turn toward it, if only Christians will stop judging them — and listen, instead, to their fears, hopes, and longings for a better world.

Whenever I discuss my faith publicly, the response is startling. When I argue that Jesus demands us to struggle for peace, to welcome the marginalized, to embrace the LGBT+ community, to reverse economic injustice, to smash down the doors of prejudice and oppression and to confront climate change, I am inundated with emails.

Not emails of anger or derision. Rather, they are missives expressing nothing less than fascination — tinged with delight — that this could be what Christianity is really about. A man as established and traditional as William Temple, who seventy-five years ago was Archbishop of Canterbury, once said, "Socialism is the economic realization of the Christian gospel." How true his words ring today.

Party politics do not have the hold they once enjoyed. Traditional notions of social action have become clouded with cynicism. In the wake of their failure, we all — like it or not — harbour a faith-shaped vacuum deep in our being. What the good Archbishop knew then, we ought to know now with even greater certainty: If Canadian churches want to fill the pews with people longing for a truly better world, if religious leaders want to become a force for change once again, the way forward is absurdly easy: Be Christian — merely Christian, no more or less — and you will, by definition, be revolutionary in the truest, most pristine sense.

Many Christians would disagree with me, of course. Indeed, there is a battle raging and roaring for the soul of Canadian Christianity — between what we can broadly describe as the Church's left and right flanks. And those on the right are winning the day.

Just a few weeks ago, Doug Ford, brother of the late Toronto mayor Rob Ford, became leader of the Ontario Progressive Conservative Party, three short months before an election that will determine the direction of Canada's most populous province. Although Mr. Ford does not appear to be religious himself, he swept to victory — employing the same divisive playbook that helped propel his brother to power in 2010, and that handed Donald Trump the White House in 2016 — with the zealous support of Christian conservatives.

Among them was Paul Melnichuk, who, in the run-up to the leadership race last month, stood on the stage of his Prayer Palace megachurch in suburban Toronto, a beaming Mr. Ford at his side, and intoned to his followers: "This is a man surely the Lord has visited in the ninth season" — the critical hour of temptation — "and granted him a dream, a vision, for the people in this land, in this province, for the glory of God."

Mr. Ford's own speech to the congregation that day, delivered in front of a giant video screen displaying the address of his website, concluded by beseeching them to "go online and register your family and friends, because that's the only way we can make a change in this province." In return for that support, he added, "I can guarantee you we'll make sure the church has a voice. All the time. All the time."

Among the promises Mr. Ford has made should that voice be unleashed in June's provincial election: to readdress if not remove the province's sex-education curriculum, which attempts to talk to students frankly, and without judgment, about sexual activity, gender identity and sexual orientation; to allow anti-abortion protesters closer access to legal clinics; to deep-six a carbon tax; and to give Christian doctors the right to refuse referrals in cases of abortion and assisted dying.

Mr. Ford's political colleagues Andrew Scheer, Leader of the federal Conservatives, and Jason Kenney, who heads the United Conservative Party in Alberta, are, unlike Mr. Ford, intensely religious — both strict Roman Catholics. Yet while they claim to respect the separation of church and state, each is viscerally uncomfortable with much of the social progress that Canadians now take for granted. The star of Ford and both these men, whether it originates in the sky above Bethlehem or not, is solidly in the ascendant.

And they are far from alone in framing the "Christian" way forward as one that veers defiantly rightward — defiantly away from, and counter to, the social liberalism of many Canadians.

Christian Elia is executive director of the Catholic Civil Rights League (CCRL), an organization that regularly defends conservative Christianity. "Actual Catholics," he says, "by following Church teaching and defending these teachings in the public square, do so because we honestly believe that we have a Christian world view shaped through 2,000 years of scriptural study, tradition and magisterial teaching that ought to be shared."

"Actual Catholics." Presumably, liberal Catholics do not qualify, being, as they are, among the very forces coalescing to ensure, in Mr. Elia's words, that "the public square is increasingly being closed off to those of us with so-called conservative, religiously formed opinions" on marriage, abortion, gay rights and assisted suicide.

Mr. Elia's is a difficult analysis to accept. Take the case of his fellow CCRL board member Tanya Granic Allen, who publicly fretted during the PC leadership debate that educating children about "anal sex" was taking their focus away from mathematics. When she ran for the Ontario PC leadership, Ms. Granic Allen was treated generously by most journalists, who gave her ample time and space to flesh out her platform, and who seldom asked challenging questions about her reactionary views on abortion rights and LGBT+ equality. Perhaps buoyed in part by that easy ride, she had the votes, come the party convention, to be a kingmaker for Mr. Ford — who is currently frontrunner to become Ontario's premier.

But we hardly need to wait for Mr. Ford's election to witness conservative Christian ideas finding their voice in Ontario politics. MPP Sam Oosterhoff, who used Facebook to denounce provincial legislation enabling same-sex couples to adopt children as "disrespectful to mothers and fathers," is already an MPP, and at the age of twenty, the youngest member of the Ontario legislature. He is also an unapologetic champion of evangelical conservatives.

Among Mr. Oosterhoff's own biggest champions is conservative Christian firebrand Charles McVety, president of Canada Christian College, and also, it turns out, another enthusiastic backer of Mr. Ford. In part because "two million Ontario children are being experimented on, as we speak, with radical gender sex education," Mr. McVety urged his followers into the public square by providing a video guide to help them complete online voter forms during the PC leadership race. Then, upon Mr. Ford's victory, he issued a tweet connecting the celestial and earthly dots as he saw them: "Praise God," he wrote, "for the incredible victory of @fordnation ..."

Mr. McVety's invitation for people of faith to inject their beliefs into politics provides a mirror, of sorts, to Christian leaders' mounting calls for politicians to openly fight for and defend issues close to the hearts

of conservative Christians. *Interim* describes itself as Canada's life and
family-issues newspaper. "Many leadership candidates and other politicians will try to court pro-life and pro-family voters indirectly," *Interim*
editor Paul Tuns says. "But these voters want someone to champion
their causes."

And Mr. Tuns finds no shortage of politicians he says are doing just
that. In Ms. Granic Allen, Mr. Ford and Mr. Kenney, as well as in former
federal Conservative leadership contenders Brad Trost and Pierre
Lemieux, Mr. Tuns says, "religious conservatives have found champions."
Champions, it seems, in something like a zero-sum game, in which social
progress is defined as defeat, plain and simple, for individual Christians.
"Many pro-life and pro-family Canadians see their way of life and their
values under attack," he says, "and they will strongly support candidates
who either share their values or simply speak up for them."

It would be wrong, however, to assume that there are no prominent
Christians in progressive circles. Ontario Premier Kathleen Wynne and her
partner are committed members of the United Church — I've preached
at their church when they were present   and Green Party Leader
Elizabeth May, were she not a politician, would likely have pursued Anglican ordination.

Still, such a public embrace of Christianity is the exception. There are
numerous Christians in political life and in the media, but it's too often
seen as gauche, politically clumsy, or plain embarrassing for progressive
believers to discuss their faith, or even simply to mention it, in the public
square.

That's partly owing to fear of blowback from a jarring coalition,
however cleft, of angry atheists and right-wing Christians. I suspect it
comes as well from a reluctance to be lumped in with American Christian
politicians and their crass obsession with what seems like perfunctory
prayer and Christian nationalism, not to mention their determination to
use the levers of political power to wage all-out war on a range of liberal

issues that even many Christians consider settled.

Too bad, because there is a middle way. Richard Coles is a Church of England priest who is openly gay and also a former member of the pop group the Communards, which had a series of hit songs in Britain in the 1980s (and whose name was a nod to the socialist revolutionaries of the Paris Commune). Hardly a typical priest, he is now a beloved BBC personality, and has never compromised on his beliefs.

"Part of my vocation," he says, is "to go to places where I can almost uniquely go because of the peculiarities of my curriculum vitae, to try to witness there to the love of Jesus Christ, to seek out those in need of his love and give them the good news and simply to be a person with a public commitment to a life of faith in a place where you don't often see it."

Nor are such more-forward-thinking Christians without friends and allies. Roman Catholicism constitutes Canada's largest Christian denomination; and while the Church remains solidly conservative on the issues of contraception, abortion and gay rights, Pope Francis is the most liberal and forward-looking pontiff in half a century — a genuine champion of the poor and dispossessed, and of planet Earth itself. The United Church, meanwhile, is decidedly on the left, a sort of liberalism or social democracy at prayer. The Anglican Church elected its first openly partnered gay bishop in 2016, and its Niagara diocese chose its first woman bishop earlier this month.

Still, forging a middle path on matters of faith and social justice — one nurtured by conversations of goodwill and openness among Christians — is anything but a given in Canada right now. The recent death of Billy Graham provided something of a test case. Known as America's Pastor, to many people, he was also Canada's Chaplain; his following in this country was enormous, and the mourning here that followed his death was sincere and widespread.

But so was the anger at anybody who exposed the man's faults. I wrote a column praising Mr. Graham's many qualities, but also pointing out that he had made repugnant anti-Semitic comments in what he thought was a private conversation with Richard Nixon in the Oval Office; had called for the bombing of civilian targets, including dikes, in North Vietnam (a war crime, by the way); was deeply opposed to Christianity's acceptance of LGBT+ people; and, at the age of ninety-three, was still campaigning against equal marriage. He had apologized for the taped "Jewish conspiracy" rubbish, and also for calling AIDS a punishment from God — but he maintained, to the end, his homophobia, his bellicosity and his rigid theology.

That, one would have thought, was sufficient grounds for at least a conversation about the man's Christian values.

Yet Mr. Graham's Canadian supporters told me in the hundreds how appalling and heretical I was. Yet, there were just as many Canadian Christians who thanked me for what I had written, who wanted the non-Christian world to know that conservatism and Christianity are not interchangeable, and who lamented that their more progressive brand of the faith was so seldom highlighted. Christianity is not united, and never has been.

But it's near impossible to see, in too many Canadian churches, the spirit and purpose of "the way" founded by a Galilean Jew living in occupied Palestine two millennia ago. Jesus himself said not a word about homosexuality or abortion, was far more concerned with justice and acceptance than with order and structure, warned the rich of the dangers of their wealth, praised and loved the poor and marginalized, and rejected the existing religious establishment. The Gospels sing rather than shout, and that song is of a shockingly different and liberated society, a world turned upside down from the one that Jesus lived in and that, in many ways, we live in still.

Conservative Christians do reach out to the poor on an individual, if not structural, basis. But for all that, they see Christian love more in terms of a moral code, emphasizing what they refer to — albeit incorrectly — as the traditional family, the sanctity of the unborn and consequent evil of abortion, the sinful nature of homosexuality, the immorality of assisted dying, the reality of spiritual warfare and the decline of Christian order and virtue.

What they lack is an understanding, or acceptance, of the need for more systemic change. Yes, they might have a deep faith that permeates all they are and do, and in that regard sometimes put other Christians to shame. Yet, underlying that absolute commitment to religion is a clinical, harsh code of right and wrong. They would do well, instead, to heed the words of Dietrich Bonhoeffer, the Lutheran martyr to Nazism: "We are not to simply bandage the wounds of victims beneath the wheels of injustice, we are to drive a spoke into the wheel itself."

Some are Protestant and embrace the literal truth of the Bible; others are Roman Catholic and look to the teachings of the Magisterium (the all-powerful teaching office of the Catholic Church). So we now have a strange unity — a strange ecumenism — where conservative Protestants and conservative Catholics have more in common with one another that they do with the liberal members of their respective churches.

This is nothing less than a startling development, one that Canadian poet and novelist Maggie Helwig, who has served as an Anglican priest in downtown Toronto since 2012, describes as "a different kind of protest movement" — one "based in a kind of panic fear about a situation in which Christianity is no longer hegemonic." The result, she says, is a theology that "mobilizes the worst authoritarian and punitive tendencies in Christian theology" in the face of what its adherents have come to define as "terrific existential danger if certain rigid boundaries are transgressed."

For liberal Christians, aware that many Canadians have come to define all Christianity as a movement propelled by rigidity and negativity, the frustration is profound.

And the challenge, says Jocelyn Bell, editor-publisher of the *United*

Church Observer, is manifold. "Liberal voices do get heard, and among them are many committed liberal Christians," she says — but those same people often do not share the fact that their opinions are informed by their faith.

Equally testing, she says, has been the passing of an era when "it was much more common for a news reporter to contact the moderator of the United Church of Canada for an opinion on an issue of national importance." The upshot, in her view? "Liberal Christian leaders today have to work harder to make sure their voices are included in the conversation."

"The scandal of the evangelical mind," in the words of Mark Noll, one of the most respected historians of the evangelical world, "is that there is not much of an evangelical mind." It wasn't always that way. The early Protestant movement prided itself on being the thinking branch of Christendom. The Puritans established universities in colonial America. And seventeenth-century British dictator Oliver Cromwell — who cut off the king's head, and banned Christmas (too wasteful, too papal) — employed faithful John Milton as one of his secretaries.

While in Catholic circles, a belief in intellectual excellence still exists (although it's far stronger among Jesuits and Dominicans), evangelical culture has retreated from the world — and, perhaps more disturbingly, is working to erect a parallel one that is run according to its own laws and logic. Which is why we see a new wave of Christian high schools and colleges, and the inevitable debates. Witness the battle between Trinity Western University in Langley, B.C., and various law societies over that Christian college's desire to start a law school whose students must agree to forgo sexual intimacy outside of heterosexual marriage.

Or take the example of the Trudeau government's decision to require groups seeking funding for the Summer Jobs Program to affirm their respect for a woman's right to choose. The decision went to the epicentre of the church-state relationship (while also, it's worth noting, making small "l" liberal Christians feel almost anonymous). An attempt to prevent tax dollars ending up in the hands of extreme anti-abortion groups was clumsily handled by the government, and thus played into the persecution complex so relished by the Christian right.

What wasn't made clear by those complaining of being victims of liberal "discrimination" was that many of these same people would be the first to refuse to hire openly gay students — or even straight students living with a partner to whom they are not married. It all seems so ugly, and lacking in the gentleness demanded by the rebel Jesus.

Indeed, perhaps nowhere is the modern-day Kulturkampf more pronounced than on the issue of abortion, a litmus test on which Catholics and evangelicals have forged a common ground against all liberal comers. It is a tragic intransigence, because here is an area where common ground is not only possible, but desirable.

All Christians, and most people for that matter, would like to see abortion rates decline. That could be achieved, and has been achieved, by making contraceptives readily available, by insisting on modern sex education in schools, by reducing poverty, by funding public daycare and by empowering women more generally.

And yet, Catholics insist on remaining opposed to "artificial contraceptives" and, alongside their Protestant allies, lead the campaign against frank and healthy sex education, while framing state-funded daycare as an attack on the family and a form of social engineering. As for abortion itself, the Christian right wants it defunded, and ultimately — however much they may deny this publicly — banned and criminalized.

For, make no mistake: Such ideological tussles are anything but abstract debates about how many angels can dance on the head of a pin. The Halton Catholic District School Board, west of Toronto, last month passed a motion that bans it from facilitating financial donations to charities that support, "either directly or indirectly, abortion, contraception, sterilization, euthanasia, or embryonic stem-cell research." Under the ban, the Hospital for Sick Children, the United Way and Doctors Without Borders would become charities non grata.

Indeed, for many Catholics, the loathing of abortion, no matter the circumstances, trumps even the most basic of Christian virtues. In 2015, in *The Prairie Messenger*, a Catholic newspaper in Western Canada, I wrote supportively about a ten-year-old Paraguayan girl who had been denied an abortion after being raped by her stepfather. I was promptly fired (albeit amid profuse apologies from my editor, who cited external pressure). Which in turn prompted Lifesite, the Canadian anti-abortion movement's most prominent media platform — and one of the most influential conservative Christian sites in the world — to announce that they were "glad that *The Prairie Messenger* will no longer be a mouthpiece for Coren's misplaced notions of compassion and love."

And yet, who is welcome at that table? Donald Trump, a man who lies on a near-daily basis, who has given comfort to racist thugs, who has admitted to sexual assault and is by all accounts an adulterer. As with Christians in the United States, conservative believers in Canada are more than happy to defend the man.

And why not, they ask. He opposes a woman's right to choose (after years of claiming otherwise), has fired every member of the Presidential Advisory Council on HIV/AIDS, has renewed his call to ban transgender citizens from serving their country in the U.S. military and has promised to vigorously appoint "pro-life judges." To a number of his religious supporters, he is a new Constantine, the deeply flawed emperor who allowed Christianity to flourish in ancient Rome: As Mr. Trump proudly champions all that is selfish and mean, these Christians accuse his opponents of being "demonic."

Liberal Christians point out the contradiction in all this. And point out, as well, the dangers of turning to Scripture as a defence of right-wing moral codes. Genesis, after all, implies that human life begins when a baby takes its first breath — after birth, of course — which is a bit tricky for the pro-life crowd. When life in the womb is referred to in the Bible, it's more figurative and communal than direct and specific, which is the case for so much in a book regarded by all serious Christians as inspired, but which many of us accept was never supposed to be read as a pedantic guide to daily living.

Or what of Christians who would deny equality to LGBT+ people — in a world where homophobia leads to persecution, family rejection, self-harm and even suicide? It's another of those subjects that, while of concern to Christians on both sides of the aisle, is hardly touched on in the Bible. The Genesis story of Sodom and Gomorrah is less about homosexuality than about hospitality — protecting one's guests and neighbours, and loving God rather than oneself. Remember, it features Lot offering up his teenage daughters to a rape mob in place of his angelic guests! Hardly family values.

When the Hebrew Scriptures — the Old Testament — do speak of homosexuality, it is condemned with other transgressions such as combining different cloths, eating the wrong foods and having sex with a woman when she is menstruating. As for St. Paul's rejection of homosexuality in the New Testament, it is concerned with straight men using boys, usually young teenagers, for loveless sex, a practice common in Greek and Roman culture. And while Jesus doesn't speak of the subject, it's worth rereading his affirming and loving response to a Roman centurion who cares deeply for his slave. Many theologians are convinced that this is an account of a gay partnership.

The progressive Christian approach is to understand Biblical teaching through the prism of love, to regard the Bible as a living document that on certain subjects speaks differently to different ages. It is to acknowledge that the writers of the Old Testament knew little if anything of committed, loving same-sex relationships. As Ms. Helwig notes, "The radical left theological tradition, which goes much further back in Christian history" imparts a message of deep humanity, one in which "we don't need to be afraid of the 'other' or, finally, of God, that God is constantly drawing us all into the vast mystery of love, and that we are, despite our many human failures, deeply, existentially safe. So we can be vulnerable, and open, and comfortable with difference and uncertainty."

"It is not the task of Christianity to provide easy answers to every question, but to make us progressively aware of a mystery," says Bishop Kallistos Ware, an English convert to Eastern Orthodoxy, and who for many years was a lecturer at Oxford University. "God is not so much the object of our knowledge as the cause of our wonder."

That wonder is troubling for the complacent, who want their faith neatly packaged in catechismal certainty. But being born again is not the same as being born yesterday, and questioning is not the same as doubting. As scientific knowledge expands and public attitudes change, Christianity today must either respond intelligently and constructively, or retreat into an ever-shrinking, more hostile ghetto.

For Canadian Christians (and here, it is not solely the conservative among them) the newest battle front is assisted dying or, as opponents prefer to call it, euthanasia. Unlike abortion and homosexuality, this is more a work in progress, a conundrum whose resolution is still undecided for many people. Not for all, however.

Last year, German Roman Catholic Cardinal Gerhard Mueller, a hero to conservative believers, paid a visit to Canada. Once here, he delivered a public speech in which he described as "tragic" Canada's moves toward a (it must be said: eminently sane, tightly controlled) policy of assisted dying. His comments were warmly lauded by the Christian right, who welcomed his introduction of moral triumphalism into an issue that is profoundly nuanced and complex.

To liberal Christians, it seemed that once again those on the right of the Church care most about people just before they are born, and just before they die. In between, not so much. In the process, those conservatives betray their indifference to economic systems that exacerbate suffering across the lion's share of our time here on Earth.

There was a time when Christian social conservatives in Canada held to an economic gospel, when they were prepared to believe that the desire for more socialistic policies was compatible with conservative views on life and sexuality. Like so much that involves benevolence and mercy, that position has been largely suffocated. As Protestant evangelicals and conservative Catholics rally round right-wing politicians, they trade away kindness and generosity in exchange for a guarantee that Canada's legislatures will call a halt to social progress.

Canadian Christianity is bisected, and — as the absolute numbers attest — in trouble. And while no faith should be measured exclusively by its headcount, without worshippers, there is no community, no money and, for that matter, no church.

The coming years will see a new generation of believers assuming positions of influence and authority in our churches and in our society. Those leaders will have the option of building walls or building bridges, of extending the circle so as to include as many people as possible or standing at the corners of their creeds and repelling all they see as a threat. Of lending a hand to the marginalized and needy, or withdrawing it once and for all.

James E. Wallis Jr. is a Christian writer and political activist, best known as the founder and editor of *Sojourners* magazine, a journal of the evangelical left. He writes: "Two of the greatest hungers in our world today are the hunger for spirituality and the hunger for social change. The connection between the two is the one the world is waiting for, especially the new generation. And the first hunger will empower the second."

Whether Canadian Christians will listen to Mr. Wallis — or, for that matter, to Jesus Christ — remains to be seen. Their decision will influence all of us, whatever our faith or lack thereof.

And it will determine whether our houses of worship, and our houses of politics, are places of division and discord — or living rooms where love is always welcome and compassion finds a home.

iPolitics, March 2, 2017

THE FAMOUS EVANGELIST Billy Graham may not have been to everyone's liking, but the man certainly tried to expunge politics — and even controversial and divisive issues — from his Christian preaching. He once said, for example, that one of his greatest regrets was being too closely identified with President Richard Nixon.

His son Franklin, however, is cut from a different cloth. Rather than distance himself from politics and sensation, he has positively embraced the divisive and the ultra-conservative. He has said that Muslims should be banned from the United States because Islam is "very evil and wicked." He's demanded that LGBT+ people be barred from churches because Satan "wants to devour our homes." And he claimed that the election of Donald Trump was due to the "hand of God" at work.

These and other comments are why Graham's appearance in Vancouver this weekend at the so-called Festival of Hope is being vociferously opposed by many local Christians. More than thirty leading Christian leaders have issued a public letter expressing profound concerns about his visit.

The list is an impressive one and includes Catholic Archbishop Michael Miller, Anglican Bishop Melissa Skelton, leaders of the United Church and (this is deeply significant) various evangelical leaders. This is arguably the first time such a broad grouping of Christian leaders has come together to stand against such a prominent co-religionist.

Having said that, an awful lot of Christians (I include myself here) see very little of the teachings of Jesus in the increasingly strident, reactionary and hysterical outpourings of the president of the Billy Graham Evangelistic Association and the charity Samaritan's Purse. (For the latter position, by the way, he is paid one million dollars a year. There's no business like the charity business.)

Yet Graham remains extremely popular and influential, with more than five million followers on his Facebook page and a sizeable base of support in Canada. It would not be at all surprising if he attracts more than 20,000 people to his proposed speech in Vancouver. His popularity is almost certainly not in spite of — but because of — the fact that he described Planned Parenthood as "Hitleristic," defended Donald Trump's immigration policy by comparing it to God using "extreme vetting" when He lets people into Heaven, and claimed that Barack Obama was controlled by dangerous Muslims and that his re-election was a sign that Americans had "turned their back on God."

He praised Vladimir Putin for "protecting Russian young people against homosexual propaganda." He calls abortion "murder" and — in sinister and hideous tones — stated in an interview that "homosexuals cannot have children ... they can take other people's children."

If Franklin Graham's opinions were coming from a secular politician, that person's career would be over. Because Graham coats his bigotry in ersatz Christianity, and because he is the son of a famous man (never underestimate the place of hereditary influence and sheer nepotism in public evangelism), he not only gets away with it — he prospers.

Sensible Christian leaders are not calling on Graham to be punished. They're merely arguing that in a country where, just weeks ago, six Muslims were murdered in Quebec City, messages of anger and discord are profoundly out of place — and extremely un-Christian.

Not everyone within the Christian community agrees. *Globe and Mail* columnist and Christian television host Lorna Dueck recently wrote that she and Graham are friends, and that while the two of them have disagreements, the controversy he generates is part of "a healthy dialogue on what the Gospel means for Canadians."

Good Lord. Truth cries out to be heard. There *is* such a thing as bad publicity — and there is also such a thing as shaming the truth of a faith whose founder preached love, justice, inclusion, acceptance, tolerance, peace, and the welcoming of the stranger.

This is the reduction of a religion of revolution and equality into a set of far-right sound bites — the life of Christ twisted into the Gospel of Trump.

I don't want Franklin Graham to be banned — but I do want him to shut up. For the sake of a fair society, for the sake of good people, and for the sake of Christianity. Amen.

iPolitics, October 16, 2017

LOOK OUT GRINCH — there's a new misanthrope in town. Speaking to the Values Voter Summit in Washington last week, President Donald Trump pushed one of the so-con Right's most reliable buttons — the so-called War On Christmas.

"They don't use the word Christmas because it is not politically correct. We're saying Merry Christmas again," Trump brayed as the gun-loving, gay-hating, born-again crowd stood up and roared its approval. Yes, it's Christmas again in Trumpland.

Personally, I hear people saying "Merry Christmas" quite a lot during the season. But the important point about Christmas is *living* it — not talking about it. And that's where Saint Donald and his flock face a few challenges.

Christmas, after all, is meant to celebrate the birth of Jesus Christ — whose politics would not have been popular at the Values Voters Summit, which invited National Rifle Association champion Dana Loesch, warmonger Oliver North, right-wing fanatic Steve Bannon, and a host of the country's other leading ultra-conservatives.

Here's the thing: Jesus was a snowflake, a virtue-signaller and a liberal.

He believed in turning the other cheek, putting down weapons, embracing one's enemies, giving away wealth, feeding the poor, welcoming foreigners and ejecting profiteers from the temple. *Ouch.*

He was especially harsh on those who had too much money. From the Letter of James: "Come now, you rich people, weep and wail for the miseries that are coming to you. Your riches have rotted, and your clothes are moth-eaten. Your gold and silver have rusted, and their rust will be evidence against you, and it will eat your flesh like fire." Again, *ouch*.

Here's Jesus in the Gospel of Matthew: "For I was hungry and you gave me something to eat, I was thirsty and you gave me something to drink, I was a stranger and you invited me in, I needed clothes and you clothed me, I was sick and you looked after me, I was in prison and you came to visit me." Make the wording a little more specific and you're looking at a demand for socialized medicine, open immigration, and the welfare state.

I happen to believe that Jesus was the Son of God, who came to change the world, liberate us from sin and bring universal peace and love. Contrary to what Trump and his followers constantly claim, I am allowed to say that — even shout it — wherever I want.

There *is* no war on Christmas in North America, no war on Christians. The former is a mere holiday, secularized by capitalism generations ago and now having as much to do with sales and Santa as with beatitudes and Bethlehem. The latter is a faith that demands personal reformation and a rejection of selfishness and worldly ambition. As such, it stands in direct contrast to Donald Trump's bombast, arrogance, aggression, dishonesty, sexual bullying and his attempts to divide people and replace informed debate with screaming platitudes.

If anything, Trump stands as the very personification of the attack on genuine Christian values and virtues — a living example of so much that the radical Jesus opposed, and for which He eventually died.

When the president told the excited, angry crowd on Friday that, "we are stopping cold the attacks on Judeo-Christian values," he was reciting a line, an empty phrase from a conservative mantra that was developed just a few years ago. The "Judeo" bit was added only relatively recently, and considering Trump's reluctance to condemn the Jew-hating Nazis in Charlottesville in August, his use of it is particularly fraudulent.

The audience drank it up because, for so many of them, the Christian faith has become a hiding place — an excuse for homophobia, racism, an obsession with violence, support for American triumphalism and adoration of the free market.

How tragic that the prince of peace has been perverted into the god of war, a champion of the poor twisted into the hero of the rich. "Not everyone who says to me, 'Lord, Lord,' will enter the kingdom of heaven, but only the one who does the will of my Father in heaven," said Jesus. "I never knew you; go away from me, you evildoers."

By the way, the original Santa, Saint Nicholas, was born in Turkey to a Greek family, and Jesus was a poor Galilean Jew. I can't imagine either of them would have been allowed entry into the U.S. these days. And as for those elves ...

ONE OF THE first things Christians are taught in catechism class is that the Son of God is not a sausage roll. It's part of a deeper theology, of course; other pastry snacks are not specified, but He is never, ever a sausage roll.

I mention this because the British bakery Greggs has just been obliged to apologize after it produced an ad depicting a nativity scene with the assorted worshippers praising not the baby Messiah but the afore mentioned sausage roll. It was part of the company's Advent calendar, entitled — with a splendidly eponymous leap of imagination — "Merry Greggmas."

Little did the good people at Greggs realize what an uproar this would cause, with the extraordinarily powerful British tabloid press joining forces with various conservative Christians to denounce yet another example of the ongoing "war on Christmas." But here, reality cries out to be heard: This was merely a slightly insensitive and crass campaign to sell meat products. More than this, there is not and never has been a war on Christmas, whether it's the appearance of Happy Holidays cards (so what?), multicultural television commercials (surely a good thing), or carol singers allegedly being banned from shopping malls (they aren't). But the sausage roll reveals a sorry irony. If there is a religious war, it is not on the season we have somewhat arbitrarily and relatively recently chosen as the date of Jesus's birth. Rather, it is an attack against the Christian, egalitarian virtues that the child and the event are supposed to epitomize — a charge led by some Christians and churches themselves.

Truth be told, some of the loudest and most active Christians tend to be socially conservative and harsh in their opinions of what is new, novel, and challenging, often obsessed with issues such as abortion and homosexuality. The latter is a subject I myself wrestled with for a long time, and I once accepted — albeit somewhat reluctantly — that same-sex marriage was forbidden in Scripture. A deeper reading of the Bible, however, and a less anachronistic grasp of its meaning, led me to question what I had considered self-evident. I also saw first-hand the love and commitment of so many same-sex couples, often Christian same-sex couples, that must lead God to smile with delight.

We must remember, however, that these are not issues that Jesus explicitly mentioned in the Bible. Yes, he did respond to the Pharisees' question about divorce by noting that marriage was between a man and a woman, but we also read of his dealings with a Roman centurion and a slave whom the said Roman loves — a romantic love, according to some textual readings. St. Paul does mention homosexuality — a word not used as it is today until the nineteenth century — but this is more about heterosexual men using boys than loving, adult relationships. And while some of the stories in the New Testament are certainly up for debate, Jesus's emphasis on refusing to judge others, especially where sexual sin is concerned, is not.

What *is* expressed repeatedly in the Gospels, however — with a virtual monomania — is love for the neighbour. Christ teaches that authentic devotion to God can only by demonstrated by this love, this fraternal romance, and such a love demands social justice, a passion for the poor and marginalized, and a revolutionary understanding of power and morality. If Jesus does condemn anyone, it is the reactionaries, those who have authority, who obscure love under law, and who disguise the kingdom behind formalities and regulations. Instead of opening the doors wide, they close them and bolt them tight.

I have no doubt that those Christians who complain about the ostensible war on Christmas and have such right-wing attitudes about so many subjects still believe in their religion, and I certainly have no right or ability to look into their souls. But it has all reached a crisis point now, particularly for those of us who embrace a more progressive, but nevertheless committed, belief in Christianity. Quite frankly, the antics of the Christian right also turn people away from Christianity, and understandably so. If that's what Jesus is about, some people say, I want nothing of it.

Don't forget that one of the leaders of the battle against this chimerical war on Christmas, and a powerful leader of North American Christianity, is Franklin Graham, the son of Billy. He believes that Islam is "very evil and wicked," admires Vladimir Putin, and demanded that LGBT+ people be barred from churches because Satan "wants to devour our homes." He also claimed that the election of Donald Trump was due to the "hand of God" at work. Imagine putting all that on a card for Santa.

What he and his friends seem to consider as Christmas is the stuff of tinselled nostalgia mingled with the self-prescribed absolute right of Christians to dominate the public square and dictate the private conscience. And if anything should anger followers of Jesus at Christmas time, it shouldn't be some irrelevant commercial for food, but rather the fact that millions of people go without food altogether; it shouldn't be that Jesus's name is taken in vain, but that His teachings are taken in vain; it shouldn't be that we don't say "Merry Christmas" as often as we did, but that we so seldom say "I forgive you," "You are loved," and "All are welcome in church." After all, per the once-ubiquitous question, "What would Jesus do?" the answer would probably be, "Tell everyone to grow up, re-read what the New Testament says, and then go and turn the world upside-down" — not just at Christmas, but every day of the year.

And while I still watch *Frosty the Snowman* every Yuletide and love the Dickensian fantasy of the season, if I forget the authentic, revolutionary, life-transforming meaning of it all, I might as well genuflect to the great sausage roll in the sky.

Toronto Star, May 16, 2018

MANY OF US had not heard of the Canada Summer Jobs program until the government decided to reform it.

It's designed to fund short-term contracts for secondary and post-secondary students and for years went largely unnoticed, until the revelation that groups opposed to abortion — some of them vehemently so — were receiving generous financial support.

A woman's right to choose, of course, is one of the fundamentals of Canada's health care, legal, and moral framework. So to correct matters, a clause was added asking applicants to attest that their "core mandate" respected Charter of Rights values.

Hardly draconian stuff. And remember, some of the groups involved compare abortion to the Holocaust, distribute flyers containing graphic and bloody images to people's homes, even when children might see them, and refer to abortion as murder. Their language is violent, extreme, and directly contrary to Canadian virtues.

Even so, there are now several legal challenges to the government, with those opposed to the amendment claiming that it's an attack on religious freedom and human rights. The actual results of the new policy, however, paint a radically different picture.

Official documents show that of the 2,728 faith-based organizations that applied for summer jobs funding this year, 58 percent were
willing to sign the attestation. Of the 115 Anglican groups that applied,
only 10 refused to sign, and only 2 of the 199 United Church-affiliated
organizations refused. Even more startling, none of the 89 Jewish or
130 Muslim groups withheld their support. Which leaves evangelical
groups and, of course, Roman Catholics.

Opposition to abortion has become an absolute of conservative
Catholic opinion even though, it should be noted, Canadian Catholics in general do not share this view and progressive Catholics have a
far more nuanced approach.

Also, there is far more ambiguity in the Catholic response to the
program than we have been led to believe. Contrary to what many critics
of the policy have claimed, of the 365 Catholic organizations applying
for funding, the overwhelming majority signed on, with less than a
third (32 percent) refusing to do so. When we break down those figures,
a clear pattern emerges.

In all of Quebec, only 9 Catholic groups refused to sign and a massive
108 agreed to the attestation. In Ontario, 63 groups refused to sign,
with 32 agreeing to do so, and the vast majority of dissenters, 52, in
Toronto. Why so many refusals from one denomination, and in one
area? The only distinguishing and exclusive feature is that Cardinal
Thomas Collins, one of the most outspoken critics of the government's
action, is the Archbishop of Toronto and represents eighty-three percent of all of the Catholic organizations that refused to sign. He recently
told a Vatican press official that, "No government has the right to have an
ideology test on anyone. That just isn't fair."

Truth cries out to be heard! If this genuinely were an ideology test,
it wouldn't have been signed by so many Roman Catholic and religious
groups. It's hard to escape the conclusion that this may have as much to

do with the imposition of authority as with an independent religious response. When the attitude of the Catholic groups not under Cardinal Collins is juxtaposed with those within his influence, the contrast is quite extraordinary.

We also need to ask whether the reason these groups refused to sign the agreement is principle, or whether some might have wanted to direct the summer program money into the very anti-abortion activities that provoked the government in the first place. If the latter, this would be extremely duplicitous behaviour.

One last point, and it involves hypocrisy. One of the rallying cries of opponents of the attestation has been that the government is indulging in discrimination. Yet how many of the organizations refusing to sign the clause would hire LGBT+ students or those in same-sex relationships or, for that matter, straight people living together outside of marriage? Judging by their records, statements, and religious ideas, very few indeed. Nobody is going to claim that the new policy has been altogether smooth, in design or implementation. But there is logic and law to its reasoning, and its opponents are, to say the least, being extremely selective with the facts.

Toronto Star, January 22, 2018

I HAD NO idea there were so many right-leaning columnists and activists in Canada who cared so passionately about human rights, and the freedom of Christians. That must be the case, because it has been impossible to pick up a newspaper or look at social media in the last few days without seeing outrage and anger at the government's reforms to the summer jobs program.

It's all largely a sham of course, just a convenient vehicle to drive at Justin Trudeau and the Liberals. The premise is that Ottawa's reform of the summer jobs program discriminates against Christians.

Prime Minister Justin Trudeau, answering questions at a town hall meeting in Lower Sackville, N.S. this month, has been criticized for restricting funding to the summer jobs program.

In fact, it's a reaction to the revelation that sizable amounts of public money were being given to militant anti-abortion groups across Canada, some of which describe women's choice as murder, compare abortion to the Holocaust, and put leaflets with bloody, graphic pictures on them through people's doors.

To prevent this, the government inserted a new statement in the application form, stating: "To be eligible, the core mandate of the organization must respect individual human rights in Canada, including the values underlying the Canadian Charter of Rights and Freedoms (Charter) as well as other rights. These include reproductive rights and the right to be free from discrimination on the basis of sex, religion, race, national or ethnic origin, colour, mental or physical disability, sexual orientation or gender identity or expression."

It's not quite as draconian as critics have been making out, and there's something else here. Many of us would like to see abortion rates reduced, but still believe that women's choice is a fundamental right and that "safe, legal, and rare" is a pretty noble aspiration. We can support this text without rejoicing at the idea of abortion; or is it that some of the groups involved want abortion to be criminalized? I can tell you from extensive personal experience that they do, even in cases of rape and incest.

Of course there are far more moderate organizations that are caught in the middle of all this, and that's a problem, but we must define who the real discriminators are. Opponents of the government have singled out the abortion issue, but many, if not most, of these same groups would not hire someone who was in a same-sex relationship.

In other words, young LGBT+ people — those most at risk of persecution, suicide attempts, and depression — will be told by those complaining of the unfairness of the new policy that they are not acceptable as employees, and this policy often extends to straight people living together outside of marriage.

They often have what are known as "morality clauses" to which they demand signatures, and I for one have been fired from a major evangelical media organization because of my support for equal marriage. So it's not quite as simple and linear as some would have you believe.

Then there is consistency. In 2010 Stephen Harper's government removed seven million dollars in funding from KAIROS, a Christian aid organization representing eleven major churches. The Conservatives claimed it was because they were reforming their foreign aid approach, but it soon became public that it was actually because they thought, wrongly, that KAIROS supported boycotts of Israel.

The Harper government also removed funding from fourteen women's groups that were pro-choice, and to Canadian organizations that included abortion as part of their maternal care policy in the developing world, even though these were often life-saving procedures. I suppose that hypocrisy shouldn't surprise us.

What does surprise, and disappoint, are how so many conservatives are playing the Christian card, and portraying the Liberals as oppressive. These same accusers have often been silent over the years when social programs are trashed, inner-city education reduced, homelessness explained away.

These are the genuine Christian issues. Abortion isn't really mentioned in the Bible, and when there is a reference it's vague and about God's communal plan rather than abortion as we know it today. Poverty, refugees, and the marginalized are constants, however, and Jesus seldom shuts up about them!

Frankly, the government has been a little clumsy in all this, and played into the hands of those who care far more about scoring points than preserving freedoms. Nobody, however, is arguing that conservative Christians shouldn't be allowed to oppose abortion and LGBT+ equality, just that financing them to do so is going too far.

Toronto Star, November 2, 2017

STARBUCKS HAS UNVEILED its new seasonal cup and this time it comes with the message "Give Good." Customers are encouraged to colour in the cardboard container and even draw some pictures on it. Oh, what fun. The banality of the slogan aside, it is what it is. A coffee cup. But just as last year and the one before, it's seen by some as the first shot in the war on Christmas, that chimera built by conservatives so that they can claim persecution and argue that their rights are being curtailed.

On an immediate level, the Christian complaint about Starbucks shouldn't concern the design of their coffee cups, but that their workers are being paid minimum wage while the company's owners and directors earn millions. And that what are often immigrants and the less privileged open stores at five a.m. and work awful hours for an income that will never pay their rent and properly feed them.

But on a grander scale it goes to the very heart of the religion-based politics that did so much to elect Donald Trump and is solidly behind Andrew Scheer at a federal level and Jason Kenney in Alberta. Put simply, the Christian right has developed a new and rather unholy trinity. They campaign and mobilize in the name of the free market, the unborn child, and homophobia.

Such a distortion of faith has always held enormous power in large parts of the United States, but has expanded to a worrying degree in Canada. Christmas is merely a battlefield of course and the war is seen as being far more long-term. One of the ironies of the yuletide moaning, however, is that it's not atheism but capitalism that has exploited Christmas and thus ripped apart its meaning. Yet that very capitalism is revered by the same people who complain about the war on Christmas.

In Canada the Christian right, while solidly economically conservative, has coalesced around issues of sex and sexuality. Oddly enough there's something decidedly pagan about the movement's obsession with these issues, and their worship of the fetus god and what they see as the virtual sanctity of procreative sex. Perhaps they've got their revolutionary Jewish thinkers mixed up — more Freud than Jesus?

The logical and moral discrepancies don't end there. That olive-skinned first-century Galilean never refers to abortion or homosexuality, seems delightfully unconcerned about how and why people make love, and is eager to understand and forgive those accused of sexual sin. But my golly, He does go on and on about social justice, the plight of the poor, the sins of the rich, the corruption of power, and that the problems of the world are hypocrisy and self-righteous religiosity.

That pristine, sparkling teaching of hope seems to have been lost somewhere along the way by many in the Church, although it's still flowing through the world's body if we look for it. Thing is, those who live the authentic message tend not to make a lot of noise about what they do.

Christianity should be defined not by what it opposes, but by what it affirms, not by its anger, but by its joy. At heart it's about a terrifying and colossally challenging reclassification of love, demanding that we embrace those who we would prefer to reject and even despise. The option of hatred is no longer available — it was thrown out 2,000 years ago, just as were the money men in the Temple.

The paradox of all this bites away at a creed that should be life changing and world transforming. As an example, I have probably learned more about my faith from gay Christians than from any other people. They've stayed true even though they've faced discrimination and sometimes worse from those around them. Yet those wonderful people who have inspired me are even now thought to be hell-bound by so many of the men and women who become visibly upset by the myth that they're not allowed to wish others Merry Christmas in November!

If the Christian right were more Christian and less right, not only would the world be a better place, but also people would have far more regard for Christians. It's surely not so difficult to understand and we shouldn't need a double espresso to grasp its truth, whatever the packaging.

iPolitics, December 20, 2018

POLITICIANS ALL OVER Canada are wishing people Happy Holidays or Merry Christmas, sending out greetings cards, and trying desperately to evince the Christmas spirit to anyone who will notice. Fair enough, I guess, but Christmas is supposed to be about the birth of Jesus. So how are these political types living up to the commands and demands of Christ, whose followers claim is the son of God, and whose name is used by Tory, Liberal, and New Democrat alike every December?

There are numerous accounts in the Gospels, those mini-biographies of Jesus, of how he wanted us to regard wealth and materialism, and how we should treat the poor. "No one can serve two masters. Either he will hate the one and love the other, or he will be devoted to the one and despise the other. You cannot serve both God and Money." Then we have, "I tell you the truth, it is hard for a rich man to enter the kingdom of heaven. Again I tell you, it is easier for a camel to go through the eye of a needle than for a rich man to enter the kingdom of God." Camels aside, when a rich man who asks Jesus how he can follow him, he is told, "Go, sell your possessions and give to the poor, and you will have treasure in heaven. Then come, follow me."

In Ontario, Doug Ford's government has: stopped any further increase in the minimum wage for the lowest-income workers; cut twenty-five million dollars to specialized school programs for those most in need; cancelled grants to the Indigenous Culture Fund and the Ontario College of Midwives; scrapped rent control for new buildings; and removed the Basic Income Project. Oh dear. Not a good score at all on the Jesus ranking.

The Prince of Peace was also pretty adamant about welcoming strangers and accepting newcomers, knowing as he did the Old Testament rule that, "When a foreigner resides among you in your land, do not mistreat them. The foreigner residing among you must be treated as your native-born. Love them as yourself."

The feds have been quite good on this one, but less so the various provincial governments, whose policies and statements have sometimes been downright xenophobic. No administration, however, has made any serious progress dealing properly with the way Canada treats Indigenous people. Remember: "The entire law is fulfilled in keeping this one command: Love your neighbour as yourself." We became neighbours, less when we moved in next door to First Nations, more when we stole their entire neighbourhood!

Peace is a recurring biblical theme, and there's not much room for manoeuvre here from He who was born in a Bethlehem manger. "Do not take revenge on someone who wrongs you. If someone strikes you on the right cheek, turn to him the other also," and, of course, "Blessed are the peacemakers." Jesus insists that we expose hypocrisy and injustice, and the Old Testament says we should turn swords into ploughshares, spears into pruning hooks, and "Nation shall not lift up sword against nation, neither shall they learn war anymore." I don't think this is reflected in selling armoured cars to Saudi Arabia, while the country bombs children in Yemen and has dissident journalists slaughtered in Turkey, or when we are extremely selective when it comes to condemning war crimes committed by foreign regimes.

The Bible repeatedly tells us to honour the world that God created, and to respect the splendour and purity of nature. We are stewards, not owners, of the planet. Yet almost every provincial leader is opposed to a carbon tax, pays little more than lip service to the horrors of climate change, and still bends the knee at the altar of fossil fuels. The environmental disaster we face is caused largely by exploitation and greed, two things Jesus exposed and opposed throughout his ministry. "Blessed are the oil magnates" is something he never said.

The verdict on all this is a little worrying. "For I was hungry and you gave me nothing to eat, I was thirsty and you gave me nothing to drink, I was a stranger and you did not invite me in, I needed clothes and you did not clothe me, I was sick and in prison and you did not look after me. ... I tell you the truth, whatever you did not do for one of the least among you, you did not do for me." For those who get this one wrong, there is the "eternal fire prepared for the devil."

Not encouraging reading for some of our elected representatives, unless they like it incredibly hot. But then, I suppose that's what spin and fake news are for. It's less certain if that will work with the Almighty.

iPolitics, May 12, 2018

I'VE KNOWN CHARLES McVety, the President of Canada Christian College, conservative Christian leader, and obsessive campaigner against almost all things progressive, for a long time.

The last time I actually saw him was on a CBC panel, when he roared against Ontario's then new sex-ed program, and I defended it. Because of that, on live national television, he said that, "Michael used to be a family man, now no longer."

He then proceeded to discuss Ben Levin, the convicted child pornographer who worked for three years for the Ontario Liberal government.

Many of the opponents of the province's sex-ed curriculum argue that Levin was responsible for the policy, when in fact it's almost identical to what is taught in most of Western Europe. It was an outrageous thing to say and do, but when I confronted McVety, he refused to apologize.

This is pretty standard operating procedure for the man who routinely accuses people of such horrors. Just this weekend on Twitter, he wrote to and of me: "I am stating the fact that you frequently defend the teaching of Ben Levin as you frequently do," and "He was convicted to three years in prison for preparing parents to offer their children for sex and his material should be expunged. Stop defending this horror."

It's difficult to know how to react to such vile polemics, and some people have recommended that I sue him, but I chose long ago to dismiss the man as a fringe fanatic, supported only by the gullible and the grim.

So it was a surprise to see McVety as a personal guest of Doug Ford — likely to be the next Premier of Ontario — in the small audience at the CityTV debate last week. When Ford was asked why he had invited McVety, the PC leader replied, "There's nothing wrong with social conservative views if respectful."

Good Lord, truth cries out to be heard! Ford had dismissed Tanya Granic Allen as the party's candidate in Mississauga Centre just days before the debate, and McVety has surely said far worse than her, which is quite the boast.

I worked at CTS (Crossroads Television System) in 2010 when McVety was taken off the air after the Canadian Broadcast Standards Council ruled that some of his comments violated their code of ethics. Even CTS, who would later fire me because I publicly defended same-sex marriage, concluded that McVety had refused to comply with their own internal guide of what's acceptable public discourse.

McVety had said at the time, "It is now a crime to speak against homosexuality," and that Ontario's sex-ed policy intended to "teach homosexuality." Untrue of course. The ruling also found that he had implied that gay men prey on children, and had made remarks that were, "excessive, inappropriate, disparaging, and abusive."

In 2011, the *National Post* and the *Toronto Sun* pulled an ad from the Institute for Canadian Values (ICV) about Ontario's sex-ed curriculum, and the *Post* even went so far as to issue an apology. The ICV was based at Canada Christian College, and very closely associated with McVety. The ad contained misleading quotes from an optional Toronto District School Board anti-homophobia curriculum, and demanded that the programme be ended. It also featured a large photograph of am obviously nervous young girl, with the caption, "Please don't confuse me." It was horribly exploitative. If only McVety's politics would stop at bizarre views about sex and sexuality, but, alas, they don't.

In 2011, he invited highly controversial Dutch politician Geert Wilders to Canada Christian College, to discuss his highly provocative views about Islam and Muslims. He said that Wilders had a great deal to teach us, "about a lack of free speech here." Wilder has called for The Qur'an to be banned; McVety has said that Islam, "is not just a religion, it's a political and cultural system as well and we know that Christians, Jews and Hindus don't have the same mandate for a hostile takeover."

This, then, is the man who the *National Post* claim will play a significant role in the Ford campaign, and who Ford himself believes, states his ideas in a "respectful" way.

McVety used to be ubiquitous on Canadian television and radio, but in recent years many media outlets seem to have become tired of the shock tactics and shallowness of the man. But he does have a following, and does enjoy financial support, and now a powerful and potentially extremely influential comrade in Doug Ford.

This weekend McVety invited people to a three-day conference entitled Answers in Genesis, led by Ken Ham, who "built a full size $120 million replica of Noah's Ark and Museum." Sounds great fun. Perhaps it's worth a visit, because if McVety achieves any power the world may well come to an abrupt and watery end.

iPolitics, December 4, 2018

SOMETIMES MAILING LISTS can be worryingly out-of-date and inaccurate. This weekend, I received an emailed letter from Charles McVety, president of Canada Christian College, addressed to "Pastor Michael." (No, I haven't suddenly been elevated to clerical status.) "I want to extend a personal invitation to you and your pastoral staff to come to the platform and pray for Premier Doug Ford at the Christmas Celebration on Sunday Night," it announced. "It is my hope that we can surround the Premier with pastors on the platform and pray for him ... After the prayer sessions and musical concert, the Premier wants to meet pastors at a reception." The letter continued with references to biblical calls to pray "for all that are in authority, that we may lead a quiet and peaceable life in all godliness and honesty."

I've a feeling I wasn't supposed to be on the list, but I'd be more than happy to pray that Doug Ford change his ways, stop making life more difficult for the poor and marginalized, and inject some civility, decorum, and moderation into Ontario politics. But my views aside, this email and the event itself — which has now led to questions from the opposition at Queen's Park — provoke some very worrying questions about the nature of the relationship between Doug Ford and one of the most high-profile and radical social conservatives in Canada.

Charles McVety is no ordinary or mainstream Christian. He has been at the centre of, and often led, many of the most unpleasant campaigns in Canada against LGBT+ equality and modern sex education, and is considered on the right-wing fringe, even within the evangelical church. He also disputes evolution, is fiercely opposed to campaigns against climate change, and wrote in 2009, "I believe this taxing and trading of air will fund the one world government of the Anti-Christ." He also has radical opinions about other faiths, once stating that, "Islam is not just a religion, it's a political and cultural system as well and we know that Christians, Jews and Hindus don't have the same mandate for a hostile takeover."

For more than twelve years, I hosted a nightly television show on CTS, a faith-based station managed by people with strong conservative beliefs. Even so, they removed his show from their lineup after the Canadian Broadcast Standards Council found it made "malevolent, insidious and conspiratorial" remarks about the gay community. I also worked at Sun News Network between 2012 and 2015, and even though that television station was vehemently conservative, it effectively banned McVety for being too extreme and even a caricature.

If his ideas are raw and harsh, his presentation of them is equally sharp. He once tweeted about me, for example: "Michael Coren defends Dr. Ben Levin's radical sex ed teaching in Toronto Star." This was because I dared to support the new sex education curriculum. Ben Levin, of course, is a convicted child pornographer. The implications were vile and hurtful.

So the litany of the man's extremism is long and proven, but while he may be outrageous in so many ways, he can't be discounted. McVety attracts numerous followers and substantial support, and his college in

Toronto is about to be replaced by a twelve acre multi-building campus in the Port of Whitby, just outside the city. It will include a 4,000-seat auditorium, 80,000 square feet of classrooms, and a number of soccer fields and basketball courts. It is also, apparently, debt-free.

For an Ontario politician who wants to mobilize his right-wing base, this is an irresistible package, and Doug Ford and his people made this abundantly obvious during the election campaign, when McVety could be seen sitting as a special guest during a public debate, and when he was invited to the ceremony when the Progressive Conservative leader was sworn into office. Some commentators have argued that Ford's jettisoning of former leadership rival and hard-right Roman Catholic Tanya Granic Allen was a sign that his interests were purely economic, and that he was indifferent to social conservatism. The coming weekend's Christmas party would indicate otherwise.

In 2006, former Tory MP Garth Turner claimed, in reference to then prime minister Stephen Harper, that McVety had once boasted: "I can pick up the phone and call Harper and I can get him in two minutes." McVety denies he ever said that, and it may not have been the case. But one wonders how long it would now take for him to reach the current premier of Ontario. Not, it would seem, very long at all.

iPolitics, October 12, 2018

THIS WEEK, THE Supreme Court of the United Kingdom ruled on an issue involving the limits of religious freedom, one that could have direct consequences in numerous other western nations, including Canada.

In a unanimous decision, Britain's highest court concluded that a Belfast bakery managed by evangelical Christians had the right to refuse to make a cake with the words "Support Gay Marriage," and reversed an earlier decision that found against the store and fined them almost $1,000.

It's not the first such clash, most of them occurring in the United States, where conservative Christians are more numerous and certainly more aggressive. This case, however, was different in tone and content. First, the owners of Ashers bakery, Daniel and Amy McArthur, presented not as raw fanatics, but as moderates looking for compromise. Second, and more important, this was said to be not about refusing to provide services for a same-sex wedding, but about not wanting to support what was defined as "a political statement."

Which is where, of course, it all becomes rather complex and messy. In 2014, Gareth Lee wanted to celebrate International Day Against

Homophobia with a cake featuring the *Sesame Street* characters Bert and Ernie supporting gay marriage. Same-sex marriage is legal in all of the United Kingdom apart from Northern Ireland. So the slogan could be interpreted as a political statement, which is a delicate subject in a region so troubled by sectarian division.

The McArthurs refused, insisting it had nothing to do with Lee being gay. Which is somewhat disingenuous, in that one's sexuality and views on marriage equality are inevitably entwined. A Belfast county court and a court of appeal both ruled that the company discriminated against Lee on the grounds of sexual orientation. The Supreme Court has decided differently, finding that the Ashers didn't refuse to fulfil Lee's order because of his sexual orientation and, therefore, there was no discrimination on those grounds.

"It is deeply humiliating, and an affront to human dignity, to deny someone a service because of that person's race, gender, disability, sexual orientation or any of the other protected personal characteristics, but that is not what happened in this case and it does the project of equal treatment no favours to seek to extend it beyond its proper scope," said the court.

"Freedom of expression, as guaranteed by article 10 of the European convention on human rights, includes the right not to express an opinion which one does not hold. This court has held that nobody should be forced to have or express a political opinion in which he does not believe. The bakers could not refuse to supply their goods to Mr. Lee because he was a gay man or supported gay marriage, but that is quite different from obliging them to supply a cake iced with a message with which they profoundly disagreed."

The case has cost hundreds of thousands of dollars, over a cake costing less than one hundred dollars. But that is not the point. As Gareth Lee said, after the ruling, "I'm very confused about what this actually means. We need certainty when you go to a business. I'm concerned that this has implications for myself and for every single person," adding that he now felt like a second-class citizen. The McArthurs, on the other hand, smiled broadly and thanked God. The Almighty was not available for comment.

But in all seriousness, there is a fundamental, even fundamentalist, disconnect between what Christianity teaches and how so many Christians behave around this subject — which, if we're honest, is not about civil and commercial rights, but the ability to discriminate against a specific group. Jesus never mentions homosexuality. Lesbianism is never referred to at all in the Old Testament. The story of Sodom concerns lack of hospitality and rejecting the stranger rather than sexuality, and the mere handful of verses from St. Paul are about straight men exploiting boys rather than loving same-sex partnerships.

Divorce, however, is indeed condemned by Christ. Would the owners of Ashers bakery have refused to bake a cake emblazoned with a pro-divorce statement, or would they have provided one with a slogan opposing same-sex marriage? As in similar cases in North America, there seems to be an obsession with one theme, one that is largely irrelevant in scripture, but indifference to the central calling of the Gospels, which is love, inclusion, and justice.

One freedom has triumphed in this ruling, but another has been defeated. Whatever the logic of the British Supreme Court, and I do not doubt their integrity and legal consistency, a mere opinion has taken precedence over an innate sexuality that has long been rejected, detested, and oppressed. Time will tell, but it's likely that equal marriage will be legal in Northern Ireland before too long. And that will be the icing on the cake.

iPolitics, March 26, 2018

CHRISTIANITY RESTS HEAVILY on the notion of redemption. We're all sinners, as it were, but we can all be saved. Which might be the get-out-of-jail-free card for President Donald Trump among conservative Christian voters.

The so-called "religious right" supported Trump in enormous numbers in 2016, even after it was revealed that he was horribly profane, and also abused his celebrity status to make unwanted sexual advances toward women. Now, following two agonizing television interviews with women who claimed to have had adulterous affairs with him, they continue to think the man a wonderful President.

In Canada, we see this to a lesser extent with the conservative Christian adoration of PC leader Doug Ford. He may not be an alleged adulterer, but his life and career are drenched in accusations of drug dealing, and the making of misleading statements and comments. His daughter Krista's participation in Lingerie Football may be irrelevant to most of us, but from other politicians such a family connection would have sent shudders through the Christian right.

So, why the consistent allegiance to such men from the usually puritanical? It won't do to merely dismiss tens of millions of people as being stupid or uninformed. Some of them might be, some simply refuse to believe the "mainstream media", and then there is the "We're-electing-a-president-not-a-pastor" defence. The latter is a dreadfully hypocritical justification of course, because these are the very first people to condemn personal indiscretions in politicians of whom they disapprove — Bill Clinton being an obvious example.

But others have adopted a specific and extraordinary defence. For them, Trump is the new Emperor Constantine, or the modern equivalent of the ancient King Cyrus. It may seem ludicrous, but these comparisons are now ubiquitous in right-leaning Christian media.

Constantine was the emperor of Rome in the early fourth century, the first emperor to convert to Christianity, whose official tolerance and support for the faith gave it enormous impetus. We're not sure when he himself became a Christian, and it could even have been as he was dying, but he was certainly a deeply flawed man. Yet whatever his faults, runs the argument, he enabled the rise of the Church.

The vehemently conservative Christian "Lifesite" media platform is a good, and Canadian, example of this approach. It ran a long article arguing the Constantine case, concluding that: "America doesn't need a president to make arguments for us. America just needs a president to give us the freedom to make our arguments without fear of being shouted down by the politically correct brigade. Whatever else you might say about Trump, he is definitely politically incorrect, and prides himself on that attribute. He refuses to back down after making controversial statements. He does not apologize for offending groups after making arguments. He stands up to the media. He is defiant in spite of being vilified by political elites, journalists, and academics."

Lifesite also happens to be one of the strongest backers of Tanya Granic Allen, the Tory leadership candidate who became the kingmaker for Doug Ford, and who is now running to become the PC candidate in Mississauga Central. The Christian right may not agree with every-thing the new Ontario Tory leader does and says, but he has promised to withdraw the province's sex education curriculum, give anti-abortion protestors closer access to clinics, and allow doctors to refuse referrals for abortion and assisted dying. Those three policies alone make the man a hero to most evangelicals and right-wing Catholics.

The other ancient used to justify support for Donald Trump is — breath-takingly — Persia's King Cyrus II, who ruled 2,500 years ago. He may have been brutal, but he also allowed the conquered Jewish people to return to Jerusalem to rebuild their temple.

Israel's newspaper of record, *Haaretz*, puts it like this: "Trump was already a hero to a wide swath of evangelicals but the role he's playing in what many believe is the fulfilment of divine prophecy has gotten him promoted to king for some of them — an ancient Persian king to be precise. For his willingness to confront conventional diplomatic wisdom, shrug off dire warnings of triggering Middle East unrest and declare Jerusalem Israel's capital, Trump is increasingly being compared by evangelicals to Persia's Cyrus the Great."

So there we have it. Whether Donald Trump, or Doug Ford, have even heard of Constantine or Cyrus is open to question. What they do know is that the Christian right is on their side, is well organized and financed, and votes in big numbers. That's more than enough for any would-be Caesar.

iPolitics, February 21, 2018

I AM SORRY for the death of Billy Graham, partly because all death involves pain and sorrow, and also because this world-famous minister and preacher certainly did a great deal of good. But he was ninety-nine years old, and lived a full and enjoyable life. I am also not at all surprised by the tributes being given to the evangelist, because he did indeed reach an enormous number of people, especially in Canada. As well as the often compelling sermons, the noted charity work, and his support for some that was progressive and good in society, there were other sides to the man.

He was long regarded as a friend of the Jewish people, largely because he was a vehement champion of Israel, and defended the Jewish state against its neighbours. But just as it's repugnant and inaccurate to say that all critics of Israel are anti-Semitic, it's similarly absurd to assume that all of that country's friends love the Jewish people. In Christian Zionist circles in particular, there are many who look to the end times, a morbid and bloody eschatology where Jew and Arab fight to the finish so as to hasten the second coming of Christ. It has little to do with Jewish safety and dignity.

This paradox was revealed in Billy Graham's case when secret tapes of his 1972 conversation with Richard Nixon came to light. "A lot of Jews are great friends of mine," he told the President. "They swarm around me and are friendly to me. Because they know that I am friendly to Israel and so forth. But they don't know how I really feel about what they're doing to this country, and I have no power and no way to handle them." He also told Nixon that there is a Jewish "stranglehold" on the media, and that it "has got to be broken or this country's going down the drain." He would later apologize for those remarks, but only when they were made public.

On homosexuality, Graham said far worse and never showed any contrition: "Let me say this loud and clear, we traffic in homosexuality at the peril of our spiritual welfare." In 1993 he stated that AIDS was a "judgment from God," and he did all he could to combat equal marriage. In 2012 in his native North Carolina he worked to amend the constitution around the marriage issue, writing that, "At 93, I never thought we would have to debate the definition of marriage. The Bible is clear — God's definition of marriage is between a man and a woman."

He condemned homosexuality as being "detestable" and "a sinister form of perversion" that destroyed civilized society, and gave his backing to the various "gay cure" therapies that have done so much damage to LGBT+ people over the years.

While he cannot be held directly responsible for his son Franklin's views, it would be naïve to deny the connection. Franklin Graham has said, "The country is imploding. We are seeing a moral implosion. Just like we saw the World Trade Centre on 9/11 when the planes hit the tower, they imploded, they fell from within, and this is what's happening to our country, we're falling within ... So many school districts now are controlled by wicked, evil people, and the gays and lesbians ... I keep bringing their name up, but they are at the forefront of this attack against Christianity in America." In 2015 he was interviewed by a Russian newspaper, and explained that Vladimir Putin was on the right track, and that the country's homophobic laws were absolutely necessary.

Billy Graham brought countless people to a deep Christian faith, and to better lives; and unlike so many other high-profile evangelists, he was not financially corrupt or vainglorious. But his theology was rigid and conservative, and he was unable or unwilling to allow experience to temper his fierce resistance to the new and non-traditional. On issues of sexuality in particular, there are too many broken relationships, too much pain and suffering, too many suicide attempts, and children thrown out of parental Christian homes, for the complete man not to be exposed. He had so much influence, and knew so many world leaders, and could have done so much better. Rest in Peace sir, but let us pray that in the afterlife you think again.

iPolitics, December 23, 2016

LIFE IS FILLED with paradox, even at a time as delightful as Christmas. When our children were small we would convince them that the NORAD Santa Claus tracker was real, and they would listen to the voice at the end of the phone — usually that of a woman serving in the U.S. Air Force — explaining the movements of St. Nicholas.

NORAD, of course, is part of the American defence network, and the U.S. military implemented a foreign policy in the Middle East that caused anarchy in Iraq, destabilized Syria and directly led to the hell of suffering that exists there now.

On Boxing Day we spend what money we have left from the previous year in mass sales, presenting an image of the most vulgar and inexorable capitalism. It's actually St. Stephen's Day, commemorating the first Christian martyr. He died for his belief in Jesus, who preached peace, love, and equality and condemned materialism and gain as immoral and un-Godly.

Three days later, on December 29, is the Feast of the Holy Innocents, when we remember King Herod massacring all the children he could find in a failed attempt to murder the infant Jesus. This comes at a time when children are still being directly targeted in Aleppo by snipers in the service of various terror factions. Generally speaking, the western world — nominally Christian — does as little as the Muslim world to try to stop the carnage.

The point is this: We've got Christmas terribly wrong, and the rot set in fairly recently. The commercialization is regrettable, but the usual moaners and religious pedants really should have a "silent night" once in a while. As for the alleged "war on Christmas," that's mostly, to quote Ebenezer, "humbug." It might be annoying for a Christmas tree to be banned or for a nativity scene to be removed from a public square, but that's hardly the stuff of persecution.

No, we got it wrong when, ironically, we thought we were getting it right. In 1914, for example, there was a temporary, but sublime Christmas truce between British and German soldiers. In 1946 Hollywood made *It's A Wonderful Life*, in which unbridled capitalism and urban development were portrayed as cruel and soulless.

It was in the 1960s that the conservative Christian world, while screaming about Christian values, wove the cross into the flag, glued God to alleged "family values" and attached Christ to an aggressive foreign policy, American exceptionalism and a suspicion of all that was not "like us."

An ugly coalition of right-wing Catholics, militant evangelicals, Fox News, Republicans, elements of the "new right" in Canada, and various influential Canadian blogs and personalities has produced an implosion. Whether they knew it or not, whether they cared or not, they've allowed a genuine war on Christmas to take place. A war not against greeting cards and carol singing, but against the quintessential virtues that are at the heart of the Christmas message.

For those of us who believe, those virtues are forgiveness, compassion, social justice, economic fairness, stewardship of the planet, care for the marginalized, empathy with the despised, a stale world turned upside down. A baby born in occupied Palestine 2,000 years ago grows up to give the ultimate answers, before being executed by the rulers — the wealthy, the privileged, the conservative, and those terrified of change and revolution.

It has long mystified me that a religion so tied to the poor and the powerless should have become — in North America in particular — so linked to the rich and the powerful. During the Christmas season that jarring reality becomes all the more obvious and disturbing.

People like to say (and a rock group once sang it) that they wish it could be Christmas every day. I agree. But what sort of Christmas? The Christmas it was supposed to have been, or the one it has become? The Christmas of suburban indifference hiding in the politics of Donald Trump and Kellie Leitch, or a Christmas layered in the teachings of the man whose birth it's supposed to celebrate?

Enjoy the holidays, and try to remember not only the people of Syria, Iraq and Egypt — and the vast majority of the world's population who live in conditions we could and would never tolerate — but also the forgotten and broken in our own country. They're the very people that baby was born to remind us of.

iPolitics, October 12, 2017

THIS WEEK, THE government of Ontario passed a law banning protests outside abortion clinics. The law creates picket-free "bubble" zones of between 50 and 150 metres around abortion facilities; inside those zones, no one can stage an anti-abortion protest, advise a woman not to get an abortion, or intimidate or interfere with people passing in and out of a clinic. The bubble expands to a full 150 metres around the homes of people who work in these clinics.

While some of these restrictions already apply, this was a long overdue move — one that gives the police more control over potentially volatile situations, and protects medical staff from having to run a gauntlet on their way to work.

A women who visits an abortion clinic is likely to be deeply apprehensive, maybe even terrified. No one in such a situation should have to cope with fundamentalist fanatics screaming at her for obtaining a legal and necessary medical procedure. In any free and civilized society, those who oppose abortion have a sacred right to their point of view. And in any free and civilized society, women have the right to control their bodies without being browbeaten by angry zealots.

As a journalist, I've reported on several such demonstrations; it's not an experience I can recommend. Those who protest outside abortion clinics tend to come from the right-wing fringes of Christianity. Their arch-conservative views go far beyond abortion; some of the opinions they express about, for example, the LGBT+ community are quite terrifying to hear.

These are the people who insist on distributing millions of leaflets showing graphic, bloody pictures of abortions — even putting them through the front door mail slots of private homes when they know that children will see them. They believe abortion is always wrong — even in cases of rape, incest or a threat to the life of the mother — and while they claim to be non-violent, it's not always easy to be convinced.

In 1992, for example, Dr. Henry Morgentaler's Toronto clinic was hit by a firebomb, following several less successful arson attacks. Morgentaler himself was repeatedly threatened with violence and even murder, and was sometimes physically attacked. In 1997, Dr. Jack Fainman — an obstetrician who performed abortions — was shot by a sniper as he sat in his living room. Winnipeg police called the sniper-style attack "terrorism against doctors." He survived, but his injuries meant that he could never work as a doctor again.

But the violence directed at abortion providers isn't limited to attempted murder. The humiliation and degradation inflicted on women outside clinics is violence of a different sort. I have watched protesters howling at vulnerable women walking into clinics, calling them "murderers" and predicting that "God will not forgive" them. Even the quiet ones hold up accusatory placards or plead with young women "not to kill your baby."

Two high-profile female anti-abortion activists in Toronto are routinely arrested for breaking existing no-protest zones, prompting conservative columnists to complain that they eventually will spend more time in prison than various murderers and rapists. Maybe that's true; if so, it's regrettable, but it's not the point. For many of these protesters, getting arrested is *exactly* what they want. One of them, Mary Wagner, actually walks into abortion clinics and tries to convince women not to continue with their procedures.

What all of these tactics have in common is an ironic obsession with "birth" over "life" — an opposition to abortion that overwhelms any commitment to human dignity. If we genuinely want to reduce abortion rates, we should make contraception free and widely available, and we should demand comprehensive, science-based sex education for our children. How tragic it is — and how telling — that both of these policies are vehemently opposed by most of those who demonstrate outside abortion clinics.

Final point: This new law is not designed to shut down debate or limit dissent. It's meant to protect women. It's hard to understand how any compassionate person could oppose that.

iPolitics, August 31, 2017

IT HAS BEEN almost four years since I left the Roman Catholic Church. There were many reasons for my move to Anglicanism, but the wedge issue was sexuality and the fact that homosexuality is still seen as sinful by conservative Christians.

My only regret is that I didn't leave earlier. My faith has blossomed without the shackles of discrimination and judgment. But I can't pretend that it was always easy. The bruising anti-gay attitudes on the Christian right are an open wound in the Church. It has seemed, however, that in North America, the Christian attitude to the LGBT+ community was reforming and softening. Perhaps celebrations were somewhat premature.

This week, more than 150 evangelical leaders issued The Nashville Statement, outlining in 14 points their commitment that marriage is "between one man and one woman" and that homosexuality is "immoral." The group behind the declaration is The Council on Biblical Manhood and Womanhood and it has influence, numbers, and money behind it. Co-founder John Piper, one of the more significant voices in the evangelical world, claims that the statement "speaks with forthright clarity, biblical conviction, gospel compassion, cultural relevance, and practical helpfulness. It will prove to be, I believe, enormously helpful for thousands of pastors and leaders hoping to give wise, biblical, and gracious guidance to their people."

Here's the problem: he may have a point when he speaks of thousands of pastors. Those who've signed on include James Dobson of Focus on the Family, Tony Perkins, president of the Family Research Council in Washington, and several members of Donald Trump's evangelical advisory board.

It's all very severe stuff but one particularly disturbing aspect of the document is Article 10:

"We affirm that it is sinful to approve of homosexual immorality or transgenderism and that such approval constitutes an essential departure from Christian faithfulness and witness. We deny that the approval of homosexual immorality or transgenderism is a matter of moral indifference about which otherwise faithful Christians should agree to disagree."

Layman's translation: anybody who is even open to discussion of gay equality is no longer a Christian, and that homophobia is now a Christian prerequisite.

This excommunicates most Archbishops of Canterbury, countless Anglicans, numerous Roman Catholic clergy and even bishops, and millions of Christians who consider themselves faithful and devout. It is nothing less than a declaration of war. This is what happens when raw literalism is empowered, and when what should be giving and inclusive is swamped by an unkind and even cruel fundamentalism.

In fact, of the 200,000 words in The New Testament a mere 40 refer to same-sex attraction and many experts question their genuine meaning. The Old Testament never refers to lesbianism, and the stories of David and Jonathan and the Roman centurion and his slave are certainly open to discussion!

The Bible does, however, obsess about the need to help the poor, fight for justice, bring peace, and fill every moment with love and charity.

As for Jesus, He doesn't mention homosexuality, but does repeatedly condemn divorce — it's interesting how many of the most strident anti-gay Christians are themselves divorced, sometimes more than once. It's as though in some morbid effort to hold on to the past and preserve a comforting patriarchy the Christian right has abandoned any sense of Jesus the revolutionary and instead cherry-picked and then misinterpreted what they find to be comfortable words and phrases. Born again has become born yesterday.

One last point. Many Canadian churches have already embraced the Nashville Statement and while they have an obvious right to hold these views, the time may have come to question their privileged status as tax-exempt institutions. This, by the way, applies to Roman Catholic churches too. If an organization is so opposed to a fundamental value of the state — the equality of sexualities — and indeed raises funds on its unconstitutional message of intolerance, why should the state feel any compunction over demanding it pay its fair share in taxes.

It's tragic that it's come to this, but in an age when the more sinister forces in society feel empowered by a sympathetic U.S. president perhaps it's inevitable. In Canada as well as Nashville.

NORTH AMERICAN CHRISTIANITY is not monolithic. That, of course, should be self-evident when we look at the number of denominations that exist. But beyond the theological differences, some profound and some bewilderingly cosmetic, there are the political divides. I've long argued that the Gospel values of justice, equality, and love should make churches natural allies with the left, but the reality is that in Canada as well as the United States, the loudest and most organized of Christians collect around conservatism.

That's vehemently the case in the U.S., and has been dragged into ever-sharper focus by the Trump White House. This President has polarized the Church as never before, and now the policy of removing children from parents who enter the country illegally has forced a visible split. Just this week more than 600 United Methodist clergy and leaders announced that they were bringing charges against Attorney General Jeff Sessions, accusing the church member of "child abuse, immorality, racial discrimination and dissemination of doctrines contrary to the standards of the doctrine of the United Methodist Church."

It's doubtful that very much will happen, as this is a church whose polity rejects central authority, but it's a powerful statement of resistance. It came after Sessions had the audacity, and the scriptural ignorance, to quote the Bible to justify his government's policies.

"I would cite you to the Apostle Paul and his clear and wise command in Romans 13, to obey the laws of the government because God has ordained them for the purpose of order," he said. "Orderly and lawful processes are good in themselves and protect the weak and lawful."

It's not only a childishly callow understanding of St. Paul's reasoning, but also reminiscent of when conservative Christians abused scripture to defend slavery and colonialism. Yet it would be naïve to assume that Sessions and Trump do not enjoy widespread support among the Christian right. Fox News host Laura Ingraham is a Catholic convert, and a major speaker at Catholic and anti-abortion events. She recently said on television, "Kids are being separated from their parents and temporarily housed in what are essentially summer camps ... the American people are footing a really big bill for what is tantamount to a slow-rolling invasion of the United States."

It will be interesting to see what Catholic bishops have to say about that, as one of their number has suggested that Catholics who carry out President Trump's policy of "zero tolerance" should face church law punishments, such as the denial of Communion. Once again, it's highly unlikely that will happen, but it does show that even church leaders who have generally been very quiet about domestic policy are at least and at last speaking out.

American Catholicism has actually been progressive on immigration for some time, partly because of its ethnic composition, but also out of genuine concern. The same applies to mainstream Protestant churches. But the eighty-one percent of white evangelicals who voted for Trump show no signs of abandoning their man, and they're joined by millions of lay Catholics who — often understandably when we look at recent history — pay no attention at all to the politics of their priests and bishops. Then there is the powerful "family values" and "pro-life" movement; it's been largely silent on this entire issue. The family only has value, it seems, when it's American!

But beyond this, there is a genuine awakening among a great number of U.S. Christians, many of whom could tolerate a Bush or a Reagan, but who have suddenly seen behind the door of conservatism and realized how challenging it is to reconcile the teachings of Jesus with the views and actions of Donald Trump and his people. He may mention the name of God and hold prayer sessions, but the face of this administration is angry rather than angelic.

Numerous Christians have long voted Democrat, but the more politicized the believer, the less likely they were to do so. Today something different is emerging. The hardcore evangelical community will remain camped where they are with the Republicans, but less committed. Traditionally right-of-centre Christians are thinking again. It's less that they're embracing the Democrat party, more that they are abandoning the Republicans.

The coming year will be difficult and challenging for the U.S. church. Christians are identifying with the "resistance" movement, asking questions of their ministers, and are in shock at this latest action in particular. The conservative electoral coalition that relied on the Christian vote is under more strain than at any time since the 1960s, and that, paradoxically, could be Donald Trump's greatest contribution to organized faith.

iPolitics, September 12, 2017

IT'S HAPPENING AGAIN. Once more, a group of conservative Christians is working to make a revolutionary faith based on social justice, egalitarianism and caring for the poor appear stale, reactionary and obsessed with how, why, and when people make love to one another.

(I'd like to write that Jesus would be turning in His grave, but those of us who believe in Christ also believe that the tortured and executed first-century Jewish preacher from despised Galilee was resurrected from the tomb. From there, he went on again to *not* address sex, abortion, contraception, pornography or any of the other topics that seem to so obsess the Christian right. Odd, that.)

The latest eruption from our local religious right involves the proposal by Trinity Western University of Langley, B.C., to establish a law school. Trinity is an evangelical college that requires students to sign a "community covenant" promising, among other things, that they will forego sex outside of marriage. And since the university does not recognize the legitimacy of same-sex marriage, this effectively prohibits gay relationships.

The Supreme Court of Canada has set aside two days this fall to hear arguments on whether law societies may refuse to accredit law students from Trinity on the grounds that the covenant violates the Charter rights of non-heterosexual students. The Ontario government is one of more than two dozen interveners in a case; Ontario's law society, along with the one in B.C., refused to license any graduates of the planned law school.

"Ontarians have a right to expect that they or their children can seek to become lawyers without facing impediments because of their religion, gender or sexual orientation," the Ontario government argues in its submission to the court.

Trinity has responded by claiming that its freedom of religion is under attack, and that refusing their students permission to practise law in B.C. and Ontario infringes on *their* Charter rights. Which is a pretty bold argument, when you think about it, since a great many supporters of Trinity Western believe the Charter to be problematic in itself — that Canada was a more just society before it existed.

Thing is, nobody is trying to prevent anyone from establishing a law school at Trinity Western, or to bar anyone from attending the place. The question is whether those future graduates should then be permitted to work as lawyers within the public square, to participate in a legal and social framework where the equality of LGBT+ people *is the law* — a fundamental human right.

Trinity's advocates respond by claiming the covenant is about protecting the sanctity of marriage, not homophobia. That's a rather disingenuous claim, to say the least. What if a heterosexual student had a sexual relationship while enrolled at the college? Would that student be expelled? Maybe forced to wear a scarlet letter?

Trinity's argument is ethically inconsistent and morally flabby — but that's not even the real problem with it. No respected law firm would hire Trinity's graduates for the obvious reason: They would be graduates of an institution that sees no problem at all in ignoring a fundamental law, and therefore could be expected to have a severely limited grasp of the law and of reality itself — to be bad lawyers, in other words.

To allow Trinity to express its prejudice in policy would be to cause unnecessary pain to its victims — and to encourage those charged with upholding the law to brazenly break it.

Prejudice is what it is, by the way, and I'm sick and tired of people trying to use and abuse Christianity to justify their own baser feelings. Homosexuality is hardly mentioned in the Bible. Jesus doesn't refer to it at all. The Old Testament never mentions lesbianism, the story of Sodom is more about rejecting the stranger than gay sex ... and let's just say that David and Jonathan might have had a tough time becoming law students at Trinity Western.

Frankly, scripture is vague on the issue. But sex and sexuality simply do not figure largely in the Bible story, particularly when Christ becomes its centre. It would make far more sense for a Christian college to have strict rules against admitting wealthy students, for example, or barring admission to people who are unforgiving, insufficiently loving, or too judgmental.

The Supreme Court will make its decision and we will all move on ... until the next Christian baker or dressmaker decides they don't want to serve gay people. In time, all of this nonsense will evaporate and bigotry will lose its ersatz religiosity.

As a Christian, however, it breaks my heart. What should be liberating and empowering is instead presented as small, dark, and monomaniacal.

It's not atheists who are pushing Christianity out of Canadian life. It's conservative Christians. May God forgive them — because for the life of me, I find it difficult to do so.

iPolitics, May 10, 2017

IN A SCENE that could have been a page torn from one of the great British writer's novels, Stephen Fry was (until recently) being investigated by the Irish police on charges of blasphemy. The case was based on remarks made by the author, actor and television personality two years ago on Irish television; if convicted, Fry could have faced a fine of 25,000 Euros.

Irish police have since halted the case (apparently, they couldn't find enough people outraged enough to file a complaint), though Fry rather hoped that they would carry on. But it speaks volumes, or perhaps bibles, that a member of the public in a modern, western, liberal, and democratic country can still initiate proceedings over being offended by comments about their God and faith.

(I should declare at this stage that I know Stephen and am immensely fond of him. But that's hardly the point.)

During the interview that started the fuss, Fry was asked what he would say if he met God after death. His reply: "How dare you create a world in which there is such misery? It's not our fault. It's not right. It's utterly, utterly evil. Why should I respect a capricious, mean-minded, stupid god who creates a world which is so full of injustice and pain?"

He continued: "Because the god who created this universe, if it was created by god, is quite clearly a maniac, an utter maniac, totally selfish. We have to spend our lives on our knees thanking him. What kind of god would do that?"

The interview has been watched online more than seven million times. I'm sure that number will continue to multiply.

As a seminarian studying for ordination to the priesthood, I can assure you that what Stephen Fry said would be a perfect starting point for a systematic theology class. He was eloquent and perceptive; his words force you to think.

I don't have to agree with him to admire him, though much of what he said was compelling. Faith is a dialogue and tough, challenging questions can't be strangled or ignored simply because they are difficult. That way lies oppression, bigotry, and intolerance.

And who knew that Ireland — a member of the European Union no less — still had blasphemy laws? This particular law is not some stale anachronism; it was passed as recently as 2009. The so-called Defamation Act prohibits the "publishing or uttering [of] matter that is grossly abusive or insulting in relation to matters sacred by any religion, thereby intentionally causing outrage among a substantial number of adherents of that religion."

Two days after the Fry debacle something far more serious occurred when Basuki Tjahaja Purnama, Jakarta's Christian governor, was sentenced to two years in prison in Indonesia for blasphemy. He was accused of insulting Islam while running for re-election, even though he has repeatedly denied the charge.

Here we have a senior politician sent to jail for allegedly making a remark about Islam, in a country with the largest Muslim population in the world, but one that claims equality for the thirteen percent of its citizens who are not Muslims.

And before we start congratulating ourselves by assuming that blasphemy laws are the preserve of a handful of national oddities, observe that such laws still exist in Scotland and Northern Ireland. Denmark — considered a model of pluralism and freedom — has just brought its first blasphemy charge in forty-six years. A staggering sixty-six percent of the Danish population supports the blasphemy law — and in case anybody assumes that this is an idea imported from the Muslim world, less than five percent of the Danish population follows Islam.

Similar laws still exist in Poland, Austria, Italy, Greece, Turkey, and Russia. In much of the Islamic world, of course, the notion of blasphemy is not only part of the political and social fabric, it can lead to deadly consequences.

In Canada blasphemous libel is, surprisingly, still a crime — but earlier this year the government announced that it was currently under review. It's difficult to imagine many Canadians supporting such a law, but polls in various northern European countries with similar values reveal surprising results.

Something deeply troubling is occurring. As freedoms expand, reactionary fears of those freedoms develop.

Insult for its own sake is childish and pointless, but strong words — to make a point or to oppose a creed — are not only acceptable, but also absolutely vital in a healthy democracy. I remember that every time I sit down to pray.

DONALD TRUMP IS a winner. Not that he's likely to win the election, but his style, approach, and entire persona are about winning. Glamour, strength, ostentatious wealth, and raw, callow gratification, be it in terms of power, sex or material.

Jesus Christ, on the other hand, was a loser. Turning the other cheek, charity, sacrifice, leaps of empathy, solidarity with the poor, barking with the underdog, and the final clawing humiliation of a criminal's agonizing death on a cross.

So at first glance it's a little difficult to understand how millions of evangelicals and conservative Roman Catholics can still be committed to Trump and ignore or justify his repugnant actions. Right-wing Christians even form much of his inner circle, and there are Christian Republicans who argue a victory for Hillary Clinton will be a triumph for the Antichrist.

But back briefly to Jesus the Loser. That claim will shock and offend some people, but the divine paradox of the despised rural Jewish preacher in occupied Palestine is that the world can only be properly understood if it is first turned upside down. There is absolutely nothing conservative, but everything revolutionary about what Jesus the Loser said and did.

How, then, do so many people who genuinely see their Christianity as the central meaning of their lives embrace a man who acts so contrary in so many ways to the basic tenets of the faith? Loath as I am to sound judgmental, I can't help thinking of the remark of the great Renaissance scholar Thomas Linacre after first reading the New Testament in the original Greek, "Either this is not the Gospel, or we are not Christians."

It's pointless trying to delicately step around reactionary sensibilities, as though every Christian conservative policy was eggshell-like in its pristine delicacy. The reality is that myriad Christians — Americans in particular, but many Canadians follow the trend — want Jesus to become more like them rather than they more like Him. Whether it be abortion, equal marriage, euthanasia, climate change, unbridled capitalism, immigration, or government intervention, they have transformed Jesus the Loser into Jesus the conservative, Jesus the businessman, Jesus the bumptious reality television personality.

They wrap the Messiah not in a funeral shroud, but a national flag, worship Him not with sorrow for their sins, but pride in their accomplishments. Once again, they don't want losers, but winners. They are instinctively conservative and suspicious of liberalism, they have embraced the conspiracy narrative about the Clintons, they associate their religion with a traditional racial and gender dominance, and they obsess about opposition to abortion and gay equality to a terrifying degree.

Actually the Bible doesn't really specifically mention abortion and speaks of homosexuality, and then deeply ambiguously, a mere four or five times. Yet both the Hebrew Scriptures and the New Testament repeatedly call for radical economic justice and the militant welcoming of the stranger. Listen to the calmer, quieter voices of many Catholic bishops and mainline Protestant church leaders and you'll hear this but, alas, the right is louder and the media lazy.

The notion of Hillary Clinton appointing Supreme Court judges who advocate reproductive choice and equal marriage appalls the Christian right, as does the liberal left's increasing rejection of American exceptionalism, which they see as prophetic. Public medicine would, they are convinced, lead to assisted dying legislation or "death panels" and any restriction on gun ownership is perceived as a dent to their freedoms, which are God-given.

They further argue that taxation and welfare are anti-Christian. This is based on a misinterpretation of the theory of predestination, and also on a misunderstanding of one or two of Jesus's parables. They seek a bellicose foreign policy partly because they confuse faith with patriotism and also due to a Christian Zionism, which is not supportive of the Jewish people but founded on a twisted vision of the end times. Wrap this up in good old-fashioned fear of change and self-interest and you have the perfect storm ... on the Sea of Galilee.

I can understand resistance to the Clintons and people feeling disenfranchised and uncertain, but for the life of me I cannot understand Christians voting for Trump. Stick with Jesus the Loser. That's the way to win.

MY BREAKFAST IS appallingly predictable and repetitive: oatmeal with hemp, and a few nuts and berries. It's supposed to be good for my cholesterol. But not, alas, especially good for my soul, and for that sort of morning spiritual sustenance I'd need something like the annual National Prayer Breakfast in Washington, the most recent of which was held last Thursday. I can only assume that my invitation was lost in the mail.

Originally started in 1953, it was always the preserve of evangelicals and conservatives, but at a time when both words signified something far more moderate. Back then it was Billy Graham who ostensibly dominated American Christianity rather than people like his extremist son Franklin, or the hysterical Jerry Falwell Jr. The most recent gathering did feature one or two progressive voices, but the theme and tone of the event is overwhelmingly traditionalist, especially when the President is a Republican, and never more so than when that Republican is Donald Trump.

He is, after all, ordained by God. We know this because Sarah Huckabee Sanders — daughter, remember, of minister turned politician

Mike Huckabee — told us so. "God," she proclaimed, "wanted Trump to become president." Thing is, I speak to the Almighty on a regular basis and she told me that she'd voted for Hillary Clinton. When I asked her why, she said it was because Bernie Sanders wasn't on the ballot.

The White House Press Secretary's consistent daftness, obfuscation, and downright dishonesty aside, Sanders did speak for millions of people when she revealed what she was convinced were the Almighty's voting choices. The eighty-one percent of white evangelicals who supported Trump agree with her. And while they might not be sophisticated, neither are they all fools. Many of them know that their man is an adulterer, a liar, often cruel, and likely personally indifferent to religious faith. But he delivers.

Two new judges appointed to the Supreme Court who are solidly anti-abortion, a ban on transgender people who want to put their lives on the line by serving in the armed forces, the overturning of a tax-code provision that prevented religious organizations from backing political candidates, and support to so-called religious freedom campaigns, meaning the rights of institutions and businesses to discriminate against LGBT+ people and claim holy justification for their bigotry.

In foreign policy there was something that many people wrongly attributed to diplomatic pressure, namely the official recognition of Jerusalem as the capital of Israel. This was designed to please evangelical Christians far more than the Jewish community. American Jews generally vote Democrat, and often take a liberal view of Israel; indeed, Jewish pro-Israel groups in the U.S. seldom made the moving of the embassy a major issue.

Christian Zionists, however, most certainly did. Their eschatological fantasies involve the return of all of the Jews to Israel, the rebuilding of the ancient Temple in Jerusalem, an end-times total war, and thus the second coming of Christ. Silly me — I thought Jesus just wanted us to love one another, be gentle and kind, turn the other cheek, and help the powerless and rejected.

Thus whatever Trump may or may not be on a personal and spiritual level, he is just what the Christian right had hoped for politically. So whenever CNN and the rest hold yet another inflated panel of angry experts incredulous at what the man has done, Trump sits back in the comfortable knowledge that evangelicals will guarantee that any Republican-primary challenger will be eviscerated, and that in election swing states such as Michigan, Florida, and Georgia their votes will likely carry the day.

It's all colossally embarrassing and shameful for those of us who try to convince an understandably sceptical world that Christianity is by its nature forward-looking and committed to social justice, and even more painful for those who are victims of Trump's policies. The Golden Rule for Trump Christians appears to be that if you've got the gold, you make the rules.

In reality none of this should come as any genuine surprise to political commentators, but it often appears that they just don't see the bigger, bible-sized picture. Proving that they should have listened to their mums ... and eaten their breakfast!

THE WORD "EVANGELICAL" comes from the Greek language, meaning "gospel" or "good news" —and up until the twentieth century, the sect was not considered to be especially conservative. Instead, these were people committed to the Christian gospel message that Jesus Christ is the saviour of humanity, and that often meant campaigns for social welfare, and against injustices such as child labour and slavery.

That's not what they're known for anymore in America. The highly active U.S. evangelical movement — with its schools, colleges, magazines, publishers, television and radio stations, enormous financial capacity, and mega-churches — has become the most influential religious group within America's mainstream body politic. Evangelicals, especially white Americans who constitute the majority, punch above their weight at the voting booth: at least one out of four voters in the past four national elections has been a white evangelical, even though they now constitute around fifteen percent of the total American population.

Since the 1960s, the Republican Party has held a monopoly on this bloc, when American Protestants rejected what they saw as the progressive and too-permissive shift of their country away from their church's values. The Democrats emphasized a new America — liberalized and more open — and so the Republicans became the only viable alternative for a group that increasingly embraced the uniquely American idea that the United States was a God-given enterprise. If the party of Eisenhower was too secular and moderate, it would have to be changed by force.

Now, it's an expected rite for Republicans to take pains to make their faith a core facet of their campaigns. Evangelicals' core political ambitions have become twinned to the Republican agenda — no abortion, no same-sex marriage, an unquestioning support of Israel that's unrelated to an actual love for the Jewish people, and the appointment of Supreme Court justices who can make these goals happen — and if those are on the docket, evangelicals are happy to vote that way. More than a third of Republicans now identify as a white evangelical.

Even Republican President Donald Trump, who has boasted of his many sins in the past, has managed to woo this group. His arrival on the scene has coincided with a shift in white evangelicals' worldview of politicians: in 2011, the Public Religion Research Institute found that thirty percent believed "an elected official can behave ethically even if they have committed transgressions in their personal life," but by 2016, that number swelled to seventy-two percent. Eighty-one percent of white evangelicals voted for Trump in the presidential election; in the 2018 midterms, effectively a report card on the presidency, seventy-five percent felt Republicans still deserved their vote.

That's about to change.

Trump, who is not an evangelical himself, but eagerly bends to their will, has delighted the old guard — but appalled their children. After the midterm elections in November, the *New York Times* took an extensive survey of young evangelicals, finding that young evangelicals are questioning the ties that bind their church and Republican politics: "Many said it had caused schisms within their families. And many described a real struggle with an administration they see as hostile to immigrants,

Muslims, LGBT+ people, and the poor. They feel it reflects a loss of humanity, which conflicts with their spiritual call."

They may not be on the political left, but they have grown up with gay friends and are aware of a tolerant culture. They have known about climate change since they were children. They defend Israel, but understand the plight of the Palestinians. And they've rejected a Fox News that screams ultra-conservatism because, put simply, young people just don't watch what has become a pulpit for Republican evangelicals.

A new generation has come of age. Generation X and millennials now make up fifty-one percent of evangelicals in America, according to Pew. Many may have been able to hold their nose under George W. Bush, but Trump, with his proud vulgarity, roaring exploitation of hatred, and execrable personal behaviour, is something altogether different. The discomfort is palpable: How, this generation asks, can the Jesus who condemned the judgmental, hung out with the poor and marginalized, never actually mentioned homosexuality or abortion, and told us that if we don't love others we won't meet God, be the Jesus of a repugnant bully who empowers racism and fascism, and splashes around in the political gutter? How can those who claim to love Him ardently and loudly be so blind to Trump's sinful foibles?

There's increasing evidence that younger evangelicals are not voting because they can't bring themselves to vote for either party. This offers an opportunity for the Democrats who, as the older generation of evangelicals inevitably passes away, could reshape the party to lure away members of this long-time Republican bloc. As Christian author Rachel Held Evans wrote, "Millennials want to be known by what we're for, not just what we're against. We don't want to choose between science and religion or between our intellectual integrity and our faith. Instead, we long for our churches to be safe places to doubt, to ask questions, and to tell the truth, even when it's uncomfortable."

And even as Trump finds strength in the white evangelical vote, the face of evangelicalism is itself changing. While seventy-six percent of evangelicals remain white, the arrival of immigrants have introduced more diverse congregants who tend to be less stridently conservative on many of these political issues. The number of non-white evangelicals is growing, from nineteen percent in 2008 to twenty-four percent in 2014.

Change is on the way, even if it's slow. But Donald Trump — a bellicose, self-styled disruptor responsible for tending to a powerful, but shrinking flock — has a habit of expediting things. And if this president's troubles continue, it could be, as Evans writes, a very uncomfortable year indeed.

Maclean's, December 27, 2017

IT'S ALWAYS COMFORTING to assume moral superiority. The Greeks did it when they lost dominance over the ancient world to the Romans; the British did the same when Washington replaced London as the centre of power. Canada has this, too. We travel, and Americans don't, we like to say; they are insular, we're not; we elect moderates and intelligent people, they don't; we're not extreme in our religion, and they are. There are elements of truth in all this — as well as risible leaps of mythology.

Certainly, in some areas, an informed criticism is in order. American Christianity, for example, is dangerously nationalistic, and the Americanization of the faith has genuinely distorted its meaning. More than eighty percent of white evangelicals voted for Donald Trump, while the Christian right leads battles against abortion rights and LGBT+ equality, and conservative Roman Catholics have proven to be enormously influential in right-wing politics and media. That's not necessarily a bad thing in itself, but while high-profile conservatives announce their Catholicism, high-profile liberals seem almost embarrassed to speak of their Catholic faith — creating a false impression of authentically Catholic Christianity. There is a vibrant Catholic as well as mainstream

Protestant left — but as is so often the way, the loudest noise comes from the shallowest end of the pool.

In Canada, meanwhile, Christian conservatives are simply not as powerful as their siblings to the south. In numbers alone, evangelicals compose around ten percent of the population of Canada, whereas more than a quarter of Americans identify as evangelical. Indeed, when it comes to the power of Canada's religious right, I once heard Ian Paisley — the late Northern Irish firebrand who, for all his bigotry, had the spark of wit — refer, in his thick Ulster accent, to Canada's evangelicals with an "emphasis on jelly." In other words, he considered the Canadian Christian right to be, well, rather Canadian in its meekness.

But the truth is that Canadian Christianity is more nuanced and less polarized than in the United States. One reason is that while Americans are rightly proud of their separation of church and state, Canada's variation is less codified and formal. Ironically, this has proven to be a liberating and empowering influence on American Christianity, as though they feel obliged to try to influence and shape the state *because* they're outside it.

Another reason is that almost forty percent of Canadians are Roman Catholic, which is both extraordinarily high and, perhaps surprisingly, trends against conservatism and uniformity. While in theory Rome doesn't tolerate theological dissent, in reality, individual Catholics have all sorts of moral and political positions. Catholicism is often cultural rather than religious, and so while bishops may make statements about public issues — usually marriage, abortion, euthanasia, or sex education — they know that they speak for a limited number of their flock.

So with the exception of a handful of hardline groups on the Catholic fringe, this leaves Christian conservative politics to Canada's evangelicals — and they've come relatively late to the game, with their origins being far from reactionary. After all, Tommy Douglas — the first leader of the New Democratic Party — was a Baptist minister.

And Canada's social democratic tradition was strongly flavoured by non-conformist Protestants, much in the way that the British Labour Party was said to owe more to Methodism than to Marx. There are also more than 200,000 Mennonites in Canada, and their Anabaptist and pacifist origins mean that while they can be conservative on certain subjects, they also embrace a powerful social-justice theology.

Still, conservative evangelicals and Catholics in Canada do champion campaigns against equal marriage, abortion rights, assisted dying, and modern sex-ed curricula. They also advocate for publicly funded faith schools, home-schooling, and so-called parental rights, referring to the conceit that Christian parents should be able to decide what their children learn at school, especially when it comes to sex, evolution, and other religions. They're also prominent in rejecting accepted wisdom concerning ecology, with polls revealing that the highest rate of denial of human-made climate change is among evangelicals.

The two most influential conservatives in Canada — Andrew Scheer and Jason Kenney — are both orthodox Catholics and owe much of their success to right-wing Christians and their well-funded, well-organized pressure groups. Even at a less senior level, the 2016 election of Sam Oosterhoff, the youngest MPP in Ontario's history, owed much to the activism and voting of the Christian right; his riding of Niagara West — Glanbrook is, after all, in the buckle of the eastern Bible belt. (The west's belt stretches across southern Alberta.)

It's also home to a vibrant and political Dutch community, an important element of Canada's religious right. The Canadian army liberated a number of Dutch cities at the end of the Second World War, and with a large Dutch population already here, immigration to Canada was inevitable. Those who came to Canada in the 1940s and '50s were both Catholic and Protestant, of the political left as well as right, but the themes of Calvinism — which emphasizes a traditional interpretation of Scripture, and the need for the faithful to be politically engaged —

were enormously strong. Many look to the inspiration of Abraham Kuyper, an early twentieth century Dutch prime minister and theologian, whose approach is summarized thus: "There is not a square inch in the whole domain of our human existence over which Christ, who is Sovereign over all, does not cry, 'Mine!'"

More recent immigration has also affected the Christian right in Canada, as political parties work to court various religious ethnic communities. While many are Muslim, those who are Christian often come from churches that are at the less progressive end of the scale, a fact that certainly hasn't escaped white conservative Christian leaders. I reported on three demonstrations against Ontario's new sex-ed curriculum, and the encouragement — or was it manipulation? — of Asian and Middle Eastern Christians by a more traditional leadership was obvious.

The enigma of this is that while any religious text is open to interpretation, the central writings of Christianity — the very handbook, if you like — are the four Gospels, and they depict a Jesus who says little and often nothing about the social, moral, and sexual issues that seem to obsess conservative Protestants and Catholics. He does, however, speak and teach consistently about the evils of social injustice, and the need to reject wealth and power and embrace the marginalized and broken. The Christian right rests its case more on the prohibitions contained in the Old Testament and in the letters of St. Paul, but often with far too little acknowledgement of their context and when they were written. Paul is simply not the misogynist or homophobe that some of his modern followers like to think he is.

It's patronizing to completely dismiss this wing of the Church. But at the same time, their monomania and approach to the Bible can be frustrating; it's a little like trying to understand a novel by only reading the semi-colons. It's also harmful because it hurts many who are already under attack, and it also makes Christianity appear loveless — even cruel.

The real testing ground for the political power of Canada's religious right will be the next federal election. In spite of what his critics might think, Stephen Harper was always careful to keep social conservatives at a certain distance. Scheer, however, is far more of a true believer, and while some of his advisors are recommending caution and his public comments suggest that he will keep his faith out of the House of Commons, this son of a Roman Catholic deacon is perceived as the great hope of the Christian right. His campaign in 2019 could be buoyed — or broken — by their support.

Then again, Lethbridge is not Alabama, Niagara is not Texas, and Canadian Christianity has no Franklin Graham or Mike Pence. When Canadians next go to the polls, it may well be the great litmus test of just how much influence religious conservatives have. The answer is probably less than they like to think — but more than the secular world thinks it likes.

SOME YEARS AGO I was asked to deliver a lecture at Wheaton College in Illinois, perhaps the premier evangelical university in North America. My particular areas of expertise were the authors C.S. Lewis and G.K. Chesterton. As it happens, beyond their genius these men were also heavy drinkers, but the college was teetotal and I had to agree not to drink any alcohol on campus or bring any onto the premises. Odd, perhaps inconsistent, even hypocritical.

I mention this because of the ongoing case of Trinity Western University in British Columbia and the evangelical Christian college's proposed law school. Various bar associations have refused to recognize any future graduates because of the college's rules about sex and effective ban on gay students. Now the Canadian Bar Association has asked for intervenor status in a case to argue against Trinity Western.

The fact that Trinity Western University in Langley, British Columbia, could demand accreditation from various bar associations while openly contradicting the very law that it is asking to teach is baffling.

The college's Community Covenant that has caused the problem speaks of Biblical principles and outlines some often entirely admirable if intrusive ways of life for students. It does, however, spend an inordinate amount of time dealing with issues of sex and while careful not to specifically name homosexuality the meaning is obvious. There are at least three references.

The first says students must "observe modesty, purity and appropriate intimacy in all relationships, reserve sexual expressions of intimacy for marriage, and within marriage take every reasonable step to resolve conflict and avoid divorce." The second forbids "sexual intimacy that violates the sacredness of marriage between a man and a woman." And a third states, "According to the Bible, sexual intimacy is reserved for marriage between one man and one woman, and within that marriage bond it is God's intention that it be enjoyed as a means for marital intimacy and procreation."

Here's where it all becomes rather murky. Jesus never even mentions homosexuality, but He does repeatedly condemn divorce in a Roman, Greek and Jewish culture that readily accepted it. So while Trinity Western — and for that matter pretty much every other evangelical university with a similar code — requests "reasonable" steps to avoid divorce it does not forbid it and divorce would be no barrier to enrolment.

It's difficult not to conclude from this that there is something of a double standard on display and perhaps even an attempt to disguise social prejudice as religious dogma. Remember, some conservative Christians also tried to use Scripture to oppose interracial marriage, to support slavery, and to fight against female equality.

The reality is that modern theology is increasingly revising the view that homosexuality is sinful and several churches in Europe and North America are not only fully accepting of openly gay people, but bless and even conduct same-sex weddings. The time when certain Christians could comfortably rely on archaic and crassly literal interpretations of words written millennia ago to bolster a reactionary attitude is long gone, and I say this as a serious and committed Christian.

As much as every Canadian has a right to object to equal marriage, to refuse to attend a same-sex wedding and, in the case of churches, to refuse to hold one, an entirely different equation applies in this case. Trinity Western wants to open a law school where they will educate Canadian lawyers, whose job is to administer and uphold Canadian law. Yet the law of Canada not only approves of same-sex marriage, but also includes legislation to protect gay people from discrimination.

Thus the fact that Trinity Western could demand accreditation from various bar associations while openly contradicting the very law that it is asking to teach is, quite frankly, baffling. More than this, while no evangelical is banned from attending a secular law school, even one with numerous gay staff and students, gay men and women are effectively banned from attending this proposed evangelical school. That's not fair, not Canadian and not the law.

The truth of the matter is that very few gay students are likely to apply to Trinity Western's law school and that many evangelicals will never change their views about homosexuality whatever the arguments and whatever the truth. But the law must apply equally to all of us whatever our faith or sexuality, and lawyers in particular must believe that sparkling reality in their minds as well as in their souls.

iPolitics, December 2, 2016

IT'S BECOMING COMMONPLACE now. The latest flap involves Chip and Joanna Gaines (who, I must admit, I'd not heard of before all this), stars of an HGTV show called *Fixer Upper*. It seems they're beloved by legions of people obsessed with home improvement.

They are also members of a homophobic evangelical church whose pastor thinks he can "convert LGBT people into being straight." The celebrity couple's views aren't known, but it's reasonable to assume they attend a church that makes them feel comfortable and affirmed.

This revelation has led to calls for a boycott, and was partly dealt with by the show's producers announcing that they would welcome a same-sex couple onto *Fixer Upper* to have their home improved. (Not, one hopes, to be prayed over so that they can be miraculously "fixed up" and become heterosexual.)

It's all rather absurd really, and the best way to deal with these people is simply to not watch their show. They have a right, as it were, to be wrong. But immediately after this story emerged, the Christian right went into overdrive — in Canada as well as in the United States — claiming that this was yet another example of persecution of Christians, that

Christians can no longer live their faith, that the state and the body politic are at war with the Church.

This claim is grotesque, irresponsible, dishonest, and exploitative. Let's be quite direct here: Christians are *not* persecuted in North America. They are persecuted in large parts of the Muslim world, China, and North Korea. As someone who has visited many of these communities I can tell you the grim facts of that persecution — of the rapes, murders, forced conversions, beatings, humiliations, and ethnic cleansing perpetrated on Christian communities.

How dare these comfortable, well-fed evangelicals and conservative Catholics claim even for a moment that they are persecuted?

What they actually mean by "persecution" is this: These days, they can't be as nasty towards gay people as they would like to be. That might sound crass, but that's really what this comes down to. A marriage commissioner who refuses to obey the law and issue licenses to same-sex couples, dressmakers who refuse to make wedding gowns for lesbians, confectioners who turn away gay couples who want a cake for their wedding, hotels denying rooms to same-sex couples, colleges insisting that their students at least pretend to be straight — it's always about discriminating against gays, and always done in the name of Christianity.

I am a Christian. It's the quintessence of my life and I like to think that, even though I'm a coward, I would die for my faith if I had to. (Frankly, I'd rather spend my last moments in bed surrounded by chocolate and beer.) What that means, however, is that I try to live by the teachings of a man who never referred to homosexuality — but was obsessed with love, justice, forgiveness, inclusion, tolerance, economic equality, and the need to turn the world upside down.

Of the 200,000 words in the New Testament, a mere 40 refer to same-sex attraction. None of them were uttered by Jesus, and many people question the genuine meaning of those references.

So this is about something other than faith. It's about abusing a religion to justify a prejudice. Remember, while Christ doesn't condemn homosexuality, He does have harsh words for divorce. Not that I'm recommending it, but do these same cake-makers and hoteliers ask their clients if they're divorced? Or if they use condoms, support abortion, or live together?

Of course not. Because this is only about one thing — homosexuality.

If you break the law, if you withhold a service or deny someone an education due to race, gender, religion, or sexuality, there are consequences. This isn't about freedom of religion. This is about equality under the law — and you have no more right to reject a same-sex couple than you do a mixed-race couple.

There are, mind you, Christians being arrested on a regular basis because they protest economic and social oppression — but they don't whine about persecution and they certainly don't have the media connections and financial clout of their conservative co-religionists. Faith has a vital part to play in politics, just as it did in the struggle against slavery and child labour and for civil rights and the welfare state.

But to wrap hatred up in the cloak of a humble and world-changing Jewish revolutionary from 2,000 years ago isn't only pernicious. It's the greatest heresy of them all.

iPolitics, January 19, 2018

THE SELF-DESCRIBED "PRO-LIFE" movement is ecstatic right now. Today, Donald Trump addresses the March for Life in Washington D.C. live by satellite from the Rose Garden — the first sitting U.S. president to do so.

Other presidents have sent their best wishes and support, or have addressed the march via telephone or a radio hook-up. Never before has the occupant of the White House made such a determined effort to show solidarity with a gathering that in past years has numbered more than 600,000 people.

March for Life President Jeanne Mancini said that "since his first day in office, President Trump has remained steadfast on his campaign promises to the pro-life cause and has actively worked to protect the unborn ... Over the past year, the Trump administration has significantly advanced pro-life policy, and it is with great confidence that, under his leadership, we expect to see other pro-life achievements in the years to come."

The moral disconnect here is staggering. Trump's numerous insulting statements about Third World countries, about refugees and immigrants, and even about reporters with physical disabilities show that he has a severely limited respect for life. His repugnant comments about women (and about sex), his ambivalence towards white supremacists and his cruel abuse of critics and rivals reveal a disregard for other people, and for basic standards of decency, that is unparalleled in American politics.

Donald Trump is not supportive of "life" in any sensible or rational sense — but he is now a vocal supporter of the pro-life movement. It's a recent position for him; not long ago he described himself as being "pro-choice in every respect."

People can change their minds about such matters, I know — but to be genuine, such a change has to have its foundation in something more substantial than a desperate desire for votes. Absolutely nothing in Trump's character or record indicates that he has undergone any serious moral transformation. If anything, his ethics and attitudes have become worse, not better, in the past year.

If this is obvious to most of us, why does the pro-life movement — composed overwhelmingly of conservative Christians — not also see the contradiction?

In fact, they do. They may often be intolerant and extreme; they're not necessarily fools. But their obsession is not with life, but with birth — they are opponents of abortion, not advocates for humanity.

It's quite simple. Pro-lifers are prepared to forgive — even to deny or ignore — Trump's degradation of women, the allegations against him of adultery and sexual assault, the credible evidence that he paid off a former porn star to conceal an affair. They're willing to wink at his bellicosity and the copious evidence of his racism — because he has won them over with his policies on abortion.

It's a deal with the devil, a political pact that likely will see Trump hold on to most of the eighty-one percent of white evangelicals, and the large majority of conservative Roman Catholics, who voted for him in 2016.

One of the many tragedies of all this is that Barack Obama, who is roundly detested by abortion foes, has a profound commitment to the Christian faith — and also wanted to reduce abortion rates. He, however, was a realist and shared Hillary Clinton's opinion that abortion should be "safe, legal, and rare." That response angers rather than satisfies March-for-Life types, who want the procedure banned and see *any* compromise as evil.

So Donald Trump — arguably the least ethical and life-embracing president in American history — has become the hero of those who parade their puritanism at every opportunity, and are the first to condemn pro-choice politicians who lead upright and principled lives.

This is a sad day for public discourse, for integrity and for the public face of Christianity. And Donald Trump must be loving every moment of it.

THE FEDERAL GOVERNMENT has announced that it is reforming the regulations through which employers hire students for the Canada Summer Jobs program. It's an effort to prevent government financial support from going to groups that oppose abortion rights and LGBT+ equality, and it comes after reports that various hardline anti-abortion groups have long been beneficiaries of the program.

Organizations applying for government support will now have to sign a statement guaranteeing that they support human rights in Canada. "To be eligible," the new policy states, "applicants will have to attest that both the job and the organization's core mandate respect individual human rights in Canada, including the values underlying the Canadian Charter of Rights and Freedoms as well as other rights."

The program itself — designed to give workplace experience and training to students aged fifteen to thirty in non-profits, the public sector and small businesses — is well worth preserving. MPs decide on funding on an individual riding basis; most of the money is allocated to non-political groups. But there have been exceptions to that rule: more than three million dollars has been channelled to anti-abortion organizations in the past five years. Most of that money (but not all of it) came from Conservative MPs' offices.

One of the groups that has been particularly successful in gaining funding through the program is the Canadian Centre for Bio-Ethical Reform. This ground was responsible for the No2Trudeau campaign — which sent hundreds of thousands of flyers to Canadian homes containing deeply disturbing, bloody and graphic images of mangled fetal body parts.

Parents complained that their small children often saw the flyers first and were sometimes traumatized. Their protests were ignored. This militant organization also holds public displays in which it juxtaposes abortion images with those of the Holocaust and the lynching of African-Americans. It describes abortion as genocide.

The group's communications director, Jonathon Van Maren, is a columnist for Lifesite News, which stated recently that Donald Trump's opponents were "satanic" and is obsessed with sinister cabals and dark conspiracy theories.

It's also morbidly concerned with what it sees as the sinister social and political influence of homosexuality. Van Maren himself wrote that "LGBT activists are already hard at work rooting out heretics in politics, media, and academia." He is now attacking the government over these changes to the summer jobs program, which should come as no surprise.

He wasn't alone. Many Conservatives joined the pile-on. "What the Liberals are doing here is terrifying," MP Candice Bergen tweeted. "No tax payers $ if you don't believe/act the way the government dictates. Sounds more like China than Canada. Thought/ belief control by the State, in its worst form. What's next for these organizations? Charitable status denied?"

Communist China routinely employs torture, ignores human rights and has executed more people than the rest of the world combined.

When I respectfully challenged Ms. Bergen on Twitter over what she said, she refused to withdraw her comparison and labelled me an extremist.

Critics also have claimed that this is all an attack on religion. That's disingenuous, to say the least. The new policy states that applicants' "core mandate" must "respect individual human rights in Canada, including the values underlying the Canadian Charter of Rights and Freedoms as well as other rights. These include reproductive rights and the right to be free from discrimination on the basis of sex, religion, race, national or ethnic origin, colour, mental or physical disability, sexual orientation, or gender identity or expression."

In other words, while abortion rights are mentioned, so is freedom of religion. The Canadian Centre for Bio-Ethical Reform and the other anti-abortion outfits that have received public financial support through this program are indeed mostly composed of ultra-conservative Christians — but the groups themselves are not specifically religious, and are not faith-based charities serving the needy. Countless religious people (myself included) are liberal in their views about life and sexuality and have nothing in common with the extreme anti-abortion culture.

In fact it's all rather simple. Nobody — thank goodness — is trying to prevent people from holding anti-abortion views and campaigning against abortion rights. This is not China, Ms. Bergen.

What the government *is* suggesting is that it's absurd for the public to directly fund and support groups that oppose the laws followed and the values held by the vast majority of Canadians. A very modest, very Canadian idea indeed.

The Globe and Mail, June 15, 2018

ON FRIDAY THE Supreme Court of Canada delivered a ruling that many conservative Christians are condemning as an attack on religious freedom and LGBT+ groups are applauding as a robust defence of civil rights and social equality. In a seven to two decision, the justices concluded that the law societies of Ontario and British Columbia have the right to deny accreditation to graduates from the proposed law school of Trinity Western University (TWU), an evangelical college in Langley, B.C. The court judged that it was "proportionate and reasonable" to limit religious rights in such a case – to guarantee the rights of gay students.

The case has its origins in TWU's plans to train law students, but at a university where a "Community Covenant" is in place. That covenant outlines some often entirely laudable, if somewhat intrusive, ways of life for students, but then spends a startling degree of time and space discussing sex and sexuality. It's euphemistic in its language, but while not explicitly referring to homosexuality, the references are inescapable. Students must "observe modesty, purity and appropriate intimacy in all relationships, reserve sexual expressions of intimacy for marriage, and within marriage take every reasonable step to resolve conflict and avoid divorce." They have to sign their names to the statement that condemns, "sexual intimacy that violates the sacredness of marriage between a man and a woman." Finally, the covenant insists that, "According to the Bible, sexual intimacy is reserved for marriage between one man and one woman, and within that marriage bond it is God's intention that it be enjoyed as a means for marital intimacy and procreation."

Law Societies in Ontario, Nova Scotia and B.C. all refused to accredit the Trinity program, but in Nova Scotia and B.C. the courts supported the university. Ontario disagreed, describing the covenant as, "deeply discriminatory to the LGBT community." Thus, the appeal to the Supreme Court and Friday's long-awaited decision.

The case has been reduced by TWU's supporters as being one of freedom of religion, but that obscures some of the realities of what this is all about. Canadians have every right to disagree with — and even campaign against — equal marriage and indeed there are still numerous churches that hold to this teaching and enjoy political and financial protection. The TWU dispute, however, is more nuanced than that.

The college can enforce their covenant and they can also teach law. What they cannot do is demand that their graduates are accredited by various provincial bar associations. This, of course, would mean that they could not work as lawyers. Not because they are conservative Christians, not because they oppose same-sex marriage, not for any of their religious beliefs. The reason is that the college that trained them — in spite of how they may try to obfuscate — refuses to accept students in what are legally recognized same-sex marriages or open gay relationships.

The legal issues aside, there is reason to question the allegedly religious underpinning of all this. Jesus never actually speaks of homosexuality, which was certainly well known and often discussed in first century Palestine. He is revolutionary in his concept of acceptance and love, and when he is presented with sexual "sin" — the story of the woman caught in adultery — his disdain is for the accusing hypocrites rather than the object of their anger.

He does, however, condemn divorce more than once, partly because it left women destitute and powerless. Yet, conservative Christian colleges that enforce morality clauses almost always take a firmer stand against potential students who may be LGBT+ than those who are divorced. In the case of TWU, it speaks of merely "reasonable" steps to avoid divorce. In other words, if you're divorced we'll find a way to accommodate you, but if your marriage is not between a man and a woman and intended for procreation, you're not welcome on the ark.

So, the consistency of the Christian argument is deeply flawed and so are the precedents. We ought to remember that some, though certainly not all, Christians used scripture to justify and defend slavery, to oppose female equality and to be on the wrong side of history on multiple occasions. I say this as a committed Christian and with a heavy heart.

The reality is that those people who wanted to qualify as lawyers at TWU will find alternative arrangements and that there will still be lawyers who oppose LGBT+ equality. But a reminder has been sent that harmful discrimination is unacceptable, even if tenuously framed in theological language. And that's rather godly.

Toronto Star, June 5, 2017

WITHIN MOMENTS OF Andrew Scheer being elected as the new leader of Canada's Conservative Party, his opponents began to criticize his opinions. That's politics of course. But this time the analysis went a little deeper.

Scheer may have said that he will not reopen debates around equal marriage or abortion, it was argued, but he doesn't believe in same-sex marriage or a woman's right to choose and that matters a great deal. And on issues such as euthanasia and trans rights, it was claimed, he will certainly be politically involved. But his defenders responded that this was an "anti-Christian" attack and that the new champion of the Tories was being condemned for his religious beliefs. Now just hold on one Bible-believing moment.

Contrary to what social conservatives have tried to tell us, there is nothing especially Christian about these issues. Jesus didn't mention homosexuality, abortion, or euthanasia but He did speak a great deal about peace, love, justice, the dangers of wealth, the sin of materialism, and a preferential regard for the poor.

So Mr. Scheer and his friends, with all due respect and humility let me take you on a magical mystery tour of what that Jesus fellow actually did say.

There was the worryingly egalitarian, "Servants are not greater than their master," and the snowflake nonsense of, "Do not judge, so that you may not be judged," and "Why do you see the speck in your neighbour's eye, but do not notice the log in your own eye?"

Then we have the lefty silliness of, "Blessed are the peacemakers, for they will be called children of God," and "Let anyone among you who is without sin be the first to throw a stone," and "How does God's love abide in anyone who has the world's goods and sees a brother or sister in need and yet refuses help?"

Moving on there is, "In the temple he found people selling cattle, sheep, and doves, and the money changers seated at their tables. Making a whip of cords, he drove all of them out of the temple. He also poured out the coins of the money changers and overturned their tables."

Not very conservative at all! Even worse there is, "Again I tell you, it is easier for a camel to go through the eye of a needle than for someone who is rich to enter the kingdom of God."

Or the nastily socialistic, "For I was hungry and you gave me food, I was thirsty and you gave me something to drink, I was a stranger and you welcomed me, I was naked and you gave me clothing, I was sick and you took care of me, I was in prison and you visited me."

So in a way we could say that every time someone on the right attacks a Liberal or New Democrat calling for a higher minimum wage, stronger welfare, increased funding of socialized medicine or an end to war, it is they who are being attacked for promoting Christian ideas.

In other words, Christianity is not what politicians who wear their faith on their sleeve have led us to believe. Both Old and New Testament scream for social and economic fairness and the story of the Christian God is a seamless garment of care, not for some, but for all, especially those least able to look after themselves.

I'm one of those odd, unfashionable people who want more and not less mingling of church and state, but a church informed by the authentic teachings of its founder and not the sex-obsessed monomania of the new Catholic and evangelical right.

Sorry Mr. Scheer, but the criticism of you had nothing to do with your faith and everything to do with your fanaticism. God bless you.

Maclean's, June 8, 2018

BACK IN 2013, I was struggling with one of the most significant decisions in my life. I was known as a conservative Roman Catholic, having written best-selling books on the subject, and been a columnist for several Catholic newspapers as well as a highly successful speaker in conservative Christian circles. As such, of course, I opposed same-sex marriage. But over the previous years, it had become harder and harder to defend that position as well as many other conservative teachings. I felt compelled to leave the Catholic Church, to make my support for equal marriage, progressive Christianity, and full LGBT+ equality public, and to suffer the severe career and personal consequences. One of the people who made that move possible — and who reminded this straight, middle-aged man that truth and love were everything — was a woman named Vicky Beeching.

She has been described in *The Guardian* as "arguably the most influential Christian of her generation," partly due to her many appearances on British television and radio, as well as her substantial following on social media. Beeching was an extremely popular singer, musician, and recording artist on the North American Christian music scene. But one of the main reasons for that prominence is that in 2014, she announced to the world — and to the evangelical Christian world, in particular — that was she gay.

Hiding her sexuality for many years had caused Beeching to develop severe health problems, and she struggled with the demons of intolerance, hatred, and enforced secrecy; within the world of North American Christian music, after all, homosexuality is considered profoundly sinful. But when she came out, her career was promptly destroyed — and to this day, she is still routinely attacked in the most severe and hurtful ways.

She's now back in London, a highly respected speaker and writer, and at forefront of reminding the conservative Christian world that Jesus preached love rather than judgment. Her long-awaited memoir, *Undivided*, comes out on June 12.

Were you surprised at the reaction from evangelical Christians to your coming out, or was it expected?

It was actually a real shock to face such vitriol and rejection from that part of the Church when I came out, back in 2014. Honestly, I'd hoped deep down that they might react differently. I knew the majority of evangelical Christians around the globe believe same-sex relationships are sinful, shameful, and wrong. But because my songs were sung in congregations around the world every Sunday, and because I was loved and respected by that entire community, I'd wondered if they might react in a slightly more open-minded way. But they didn't.

How did that negative reaction make you feel?

It was immensely painful. Almost all the evangelicals I'd known and worked with told me I was "choosing sin" and stepping away from God in my decision to come out. They also told me I was no longer welcome to sing, or speak, or continue in any of the leadership roles I'd held at evangelical conferences and events. It was extremely damaging to my mental health to feel so excluded from my former community, as they'd felt like family to me since childhood.

Have you ever wished you'd remained silent?

No, I have absolutely no regrets about coming out. It's incredibly healing and liberating to be my authentic self at last. I was thirty-five when I came out, so it took a long time to find the courage. The cost was high though; I lost my career in Christian music, my livelihood and financial security, and my sense of belonging within the evangelical world. But overall, it was absolutely worth it. The fear I battled every day was so intense and the toll it was taking was too great — I had to step into the freedom of being the person I was meant to be.

You've been interviewed many times about what happened, but why write this book?

A publisher approached me and said they'd like me to tell my story in more detail, as they believed it could help others walking through similar challenges. So I signed with HarperCollins and began writing the memoir. My goal was to write the book that I'd needed, back when I was a teenager or in my twenties — a book that could've helped me choose a more authentic and less fearful path. Beyond that, I also hope it's a book that appeals to anyone and everyone, as it deals with broad themes like facing your fears, choosing to be authentic, and learning that vulnerability is actually a strength. It's a book for anyone who wants to become more fully alive.

What does your life look like now, four years on from your coming-out announcement?

It's been a huge change. My former job as a singer and recording artist, working in churches in the U.K., the U.S., and Canada, is over. I haven't played music or sung publicly since I came out. I had to totally re-imagine what I wanted to do with my life when I was no longer welcome to lead worship anymore. Now, my work centres around writing and speaking, much of which is focused on LGBT+ equality and mental health awareness. I speak in a lot of corporate environments, helping companies become more skilled at making LGBT+ staff feel welcome and safe. I also work with pastors and churches, helping them step towards LGBT+ inclusion in their congregations. Often I pop up on radio or TV here in the U.K., sharing my perspective on these topics when they come up in the news. I'm also doing a part-time Ph.D. too, as I am a geek who loves to study! Overall that makes for a very varied portfolio of work, as I rebuild a new career to replace the one I lost in church music.

The Pope allegedly said recently that he believes God creates some people to be gay—what did you think about that?

It's wonderful that the Pope might genuinely hold that view, but at the same time, it's something spoken behind closed doors while the official teaching of the Catholic church remains unchanged. That makes it painful for those of us who are waiting for official teachings to change and creates a strange tension where one thing is said privately, but a different thing is preached publicly from the pulpit. It feels disingenuous and damaging, as we are left in limbo, unsure of what the Church truly thinks.

In your book, you write that you're still a believer in the Christian faith, and still love the Church, despite its failings. What are your hopes for the future of Christianity and LGBT+ equality?

I think there's a long road ahead before we see major change. In the Church of England, for example, same-sex marriages are not permitted to take place within their buildings. Also, if you are a priest or a Bishop, you are barred from entering a same-sex marriage yourself. You can only enter a civil partnership, and you must vow to remain celibate within it. The Archbishop of Canterbury has spoken about the "stunning quality" of some gay couples' relationships, but any official change seems a long way off. I remain hopeful though! The global church changed its mind when it formerly opposed William Wilberforce and the ending of slavery. The Church also changed its mind when it previously opposed the suffragettes and the right of women to vote. Eventually, we'll see that same equality and social justice extended to people who are LGBT+ — and I'll do all I can to play my small part in moving the Church toward that goal. I hope my book can help change minds and hearts and bring greater awareness. LGBT+ equality is not something the Church can ignore. I hope books like mine can help spark the conversation and change minds and hearts.

CBC, April 18, 2018

PARENTAL LOVE OF a child is one of the strongest, most poignant emotions known. It is visceral, inexorable, even exquisitely irrational. So it's difficult to imagine just what Tom Evans, and Kate James, the parents of twenty-three-month-old Alfie Evans are feeling right now. Alfie passed away early Saturday, nearly a week after his life support was withdrawn.

Their baby spent most of his life dependent on mechanical ventilation, in a neonatal intensive care unit in a Liverpool hospital in England. He suffered from a progressive neurodegenerative disorder, one so rare that it hasn't yet been labelled, and may even be referred to by Alfie Evans's name in the future. It decayed his brain to such an extent that he was in a semi-vegetative state. He also became, tragically, a figure of world debate and discussion.

After months of care and intervention, and with evident sorrow and regret, the hospital finally decided to withdraw treatment, thus allowing Alfie to die. Doctors argued that further medical intervention would be pointless and cruel. This is, alas, far from unique; there comes a time when babies, children and adults in such wretched conditions simply have no future.

Alfie's parents, however, wanted to take their baby out of the country for further treatment and so, they took their case to the courts.

The family division of the high court rejected multiple legal challenges, and so on Monday, Alfie was detached from his ventilator with a palliative care team ready to ensure his comfort.

There were two equally compelling narratives here: that of the parents of baby Alfie, who were of course desperate not to let go of their child, and that of the doctors and nurses, who cared for the boy for so long, and who spend every moment of their working lives giving aid and comfort to the sick and dying. Put simply, there were no bad guys among those directly involved.

Where genuine love and commitment may perhaps be questioned is in the wider discussion and activism around the case. The Roman Catholic Church, in Britain and internationally, had made this their latest cause célèbre. Alfie had been given Italian citizenship, and a request had been made to fly him to Bambino Gesù, a pediatric hospital in the Vatican. The Pope even put a military helicopter on standby to bring the boy to Rome.

IT WAS A campaign that had not gone unnoticed by the Church's critics. While the Church has been largely consistent in its defence of individual vulnerable life in such cases, it appears highly selective when it comes to human suffering. When the Catholic Church in England, Scotland, and Ireland was asked to admit and apologize for its generations of sexual and physical abuse, for example, it took years of campaigning and countless legal cases for contrition and compensation to be offered. Now, however, the Church moves with lightning speed.

Beyond organized conservative Christianity, the reaction of many on the political right has been equally disturbing. Commentators who have shown no support for — or even opposed — public medicine were suddenly crying out for state support for the life of a dying baby.

Former Arkansas governor Mike Huckabee, who, for example, opposes insurance for people with pre-existing conditions, commented that, "Brits have decided some kids just aren't worth that much and are disposable." Former Republican presidential candidate Ted Cruz, once described so wonderfully as a "sad vampire," and who campaigned to raise the age of Medicare eligibility so as to save money, explained that, "It is a grim reminder that systems of socialized medicine like the National Health Service (NHS) vest the state with power over human lives, transforming citizens into subjects." Truth cries out to be heard.

Actually, the NHS spent a fortune to make sure that Alfie remained alive for as long as he did and received the best and most modern care available. All of this through the type of socialized medical service that many of this child's recent advocates so oppose. In the United States, a family such as Alfie's would never have had the financial resources or insurance coverage necessary to receive such exemplary care.

The reality, in Britain, Canada, and elsewhere, is that parents and doctors do usually concur in such dreadful situations, and their pain is mutual and shared. It's incredibly unusual for the courts to be used, and when that happens, judges hear expert opinions from all concerned and come to informed decisions. That is what has happened here, with numerous doctors from many countries agreeing that the child's illness was terminal.

It was no longer about trying to prolong life, but making sure that death is as gentle and painless as possible. Those who argue that the parents should have the final say in all this forget that without hospital facilities, what remained of this child's short life could have been extremely unpleasant, and his death terrible. Parents have a duty to provide care, even in such challenging circumstances, and in Alfie's situation could not do so alone.

Even so, Alfie's doctors still received death threats, with crowds assembled outside the hospital to protest, block vital roads and even try to storm the doors. There was a mob-like anger on display, partly fuelled by tabloid hysteria and online talk of the hospital wanting to perform "a court-ordered execution."

We saw something similar with another baby in England, Charlie Gard, and with the Terri Schiavo case in the United States in 2005. But in many cases involving their most vocal defenders, it was less concern for a vulnerable and suffering human being than religious and political extremism, and an attempt to appear noble by seeing callousness in others.

There was never going to be a happy ending to all this, but perhaps there is a lesson to be learned. Sometimes suffering is inevitable, but exploitation of that suffering is not. Shame on those who fail to see it.

United Church Observer, February 2017

I ONCE WORKED with a delightful, if earnest, young man from a strict Calvinist background who lived his faith in a manner that often did me shame. He saw the entire world through the prism of Christianity, and while this sometimes irritated an old cynic like me, it could also be downright inspiring. He took the Ten Commandments very seriously indeed, but when it came to the third — not taking God's name in vain — he could be a little pedantic. Which is a kind way of saying he was obsessive. He would twist and reshape the language to avoid using "God" in any form that might be even tentatively disrespectful.

I can't help thinking that this is not what we're being warned about in the books of Exodus and Deuteronomy, where the commandments are listed. Obviously the third commandment is about respect and reverence for God, but language is a means and not an end. In other words, how we communicate does matter, but how we act matters so much more. Expletives are regrettable; evil is inexcusable.

So, for example, we have countless conservative Roman Catholics and evangelicals using God's name to justify discrimination against LGBT+ people. From denying equality to refusing to bake a cake for a same-sex wedding, the Christian right seems to view excluding the queer community in the name of God as a virtual sacrament.

Then there are zealots holding banners and placards outside abortion clinics. These men and women repeatedly and aggressively take God's name in vain as they shout and try to shame and humiliate the women walking past who have just made one of the hardest decisions of their lives.

Or we have the appalling exploitation of God's name when opponents of any form of assisted dying insist that those in agony and despair have no right to decide the time and means of their passing because God is opposed to this.

Invasions of other countries, forced conversions and even ethnic cleansing — all manner of atrocities have been committed in the name of the Lord.

Pretending that climate change isn't real, while claiming all such concerns are pagan and God is in command, endangers not only our ecosystem, but our very survival on this planet.

Proclaiming unbridled capitalism as "God's will" and rejecting social democracy as "un-Christian"; persecuting religious minorities and restricting freedoms — all are defended in the name of the Almighty.

These, all of these, are the taking of God's name in vain. God is love, and while a moral code is vital and Christ's teachings do not lack judgment, we diminish the greatness and goodness of the Creator if we think that using God's name in a meaningless phrase is what this is really all about.

In the name of God, we have to do better. God help us, we have failed. For God's sake, we need to get it right in the future. And, oh my God, what the hell is wrong with Christianity when it doesn't see this? So I'm probably damned, but so be it.

United Church Observer, March 2017

AT THE END of 2017, the New Zealand singer Lorde suddenly became known not only for her music, but for her opinions. After hearing from various supporters of the Boycott, Divestment, Sanctions (BDS) movement, who work to change Israeli policy, especially around the country's settlements in the West Bank, the twenty-one-year-old musician decided to cancel her proposed concert in Tel Aviv.

Within a few days, a full-page ad appeared in the *Washington Post*, accusing her of bigotry and of participating in a culture of "Jew hatred." It was harsh and unfair, and indeed the Jewish community in New Zealand condemned its tone and approach. But many others rushed to justify the ad and further attack Lorde and the BDS movement.

So how should Christians react to this? What should be the attitude to an issue that, whatever zealots on both sides may argue, is complex and nuanced? The United Church calls on members "to become involved in the search for a just peace between Palestinians and Israelis by contributing to the end of the occupation of the Palestinian Territories." It agrees with most of the international community in believing the settlements to be illegal, and in 2015 its forty-second General Council passed a motion encouraging divestment "against all corporations and institutions complicit in and benefitting from the illegal occupation."

A few facts. First, the Jewish people have suffered almost unparalleled persecution throughout their history, often at the hands of alleged Christians. Jews did not leave the European homes they had known for centuries for the Middle East just for fun. Never forget the blood libels, the pogroms, and the Holocaust. And if you think anti-Semitism is of the past, I'd invite you to spend some time on this half-Jewish writer's social media feeds!

Second, the notion that Israel was a land without people given to a people without land is a myth. While the Jews have a historic attachment to Israel, so do the Palestinians. Arab Muslims and Christians — and Jews for that matter — lived in sizable numbers in the region long before the first waves of Jewish immigration in the nineteenth century and the establishment of Israel in 1948.

As for the boycotts, that should be left to each person to decide. There are opponents of Israeli policy who disagree with the BDS movement, and others who actively support it. One of the most prominent of the latter is British musician Brian Eno. He told me recently, "I'm not in it for a fight with Israel, but for a result for everyone. I really think there are a lot of people on both sides who prefer the fighting to the result-getting — especially if the 'fighting' is being done from the cozy comfort of a computer."

Quite so. Sweeping generalizations are easy and dangerous. Informed and sensible efforts to bring peace and coexistence to two valid, but clashing narratives are much more difficult — but much more necessary.

United Church Observer, July 2018

THIS APRIL, A massacre occurred in Toronto when a van was driven through crowded sidewalks, killing ten people and injuring sixteen. What can be said about such a grotesque, pointless crime? That our thoughts and prayers are with the victims, that we are in shock or tears, that we should all hug one another? Much of that might be true, but I'm not sure what is achieved by making our feelings so public. It's easy to play the cynic in this, but the one absolute is that it's the dead, the wounded, and their loved ones who matter. The rest of us are simply not the story.

I reported from Northern Ireland more than thirty years ago and saw violence and suffering first-hand. On one occasion, someone was shot dead just a few steps away from me. It took almost forty-eight hours for me to react, and when I did I sat in my hotel room and sobbed. As awful as this experience was, however, life did reset astoundingly quickly.

So when reporters constantly ask people with no direct involvement how they feel and demand to know what the traumatic event means to them, we must ask whether this is easing the situation, aiding the victims, or merely magnifying public emotion for its own sake. Of course I care, of course I feel, but I'm not sure if genuine compassion and meaningful empathy are helped or hindered by this culture of public grieving.

When Princess Diana died in 1997, for example, Britain sank into paroxysms of sorrow. It was indeed terrible that a young woman, a mother of small children, should die like that. But this mass reaction was for someone most people had never met and knew only through media. I hosted a radio show at the time, and while expressing sympathy for Diana and her family, mentioned a recent story about a person from London who had died in their home, and none of the neighbours even noticed for almost a month. Real community, I suggested, is about caring for all and not concentrating love on one lionized figure.

The Toronto horror and other attacks are different from the death of Diana, of course, but our reaction to them still provokes some questions: Do we react the same way when countless innocent people are murdered in the Middle East? Do we show such emotion when yet another homeless person dies? I think we know the answer.

Part of the problem is that we've forgotten how to grieve. The decline of organized religion has removed much of that collective solidarity, whether it's the Roman Catholic wake, the Jewish shiva, or any other ordered process of trying to deal with passing. Public vigils do take place, of course — and the one in Toronto brought various faith leaders together — but while the intentions are noble, the results are often varied. Remember, cameras abound, and there is "being at a happening" as well as genuine mourning taking place.

Please grieve, please feel, and please share in the pain of others. But for all people. And never forget that it's never about us; it's always about them.

United Church Observer, October 2017

BACK IN JULY, the Omar Khadr case became a national controversy. For those who've forgotten, Khadr, a Canadian, was taken as a boy by his father to Afghanistan, where he fought and was wounded. He was captured, delivered to Guantanamo Bay by the Americans, and tortured. Then he confessed — his lawyers say under duress — to throwing a grenade that killed an American soldier.

He later said he doesn't know if he threw the grenade, so we have no idea if that actually happened. What we do know is that the Canadian government did nothing to prevent his incarceration and mistreatment, and that our Supreme Court ruled his rights had been denied and he was owed an apology. Prime Minister Justin Trudeau did apologize and also provided ten and a half million dollars in compensation, most of which is likely to go to Khadr's lawyers.

So much was written at the time about the case that I will not reiterate the arguments now. I believe the government acted properly, and that one can detest jihadist terrorism and still support Khadr.

What interests me now is the profoundly angry reaction from many Christians. From senior politicians to social media warriors, legions of people who describe themselves as orthodox Roman Catholics, Christian patriots, evangelicals and the like accused those who were sympathetic to Khadr as being supporters of terrorism, of not caring about the family of the deceased soldier, of being in favour of Islamic radicalism and of insulting our own military. (By contrast, The United Church of Canada released a statement that said it "respects" the federal government's decision to apologize to Khadr.)

There was certainly room for civilized disagreement over what happened, but this was not the spirit of the debate at all. It was no longer right and wrong, but good and bad. I certainly felt the sting of accusation from countless conservative Christians, and I couldn't help but think of the prayer of St. Francis: "Lord, make me an instrument of your peace: where there is hatred, let me sow love; where there is injury, pardon," and so on.

I realize that politics doesn't always lead to easy and comfortable consensus, but I am convinced that the damage done to informed and respectful debate by social media and twenty-four-hour news has inflicted colossal damage on the Christian conversation.

When we are astounded, upset or even hurt by something that is said, we too often reject the speaker rather than the argument. That's bad enough in secular life. But if we are convinced that everybody is made in the image of God, how dare we act this way? Instead of trying to find the possible merits of an opposing opinion or understand the reasons why the argument was made in the first place, we reduce it to a caricature and then attribute base motives.

We must do better.

And no, that's not me being Pollyanna. That's me trying to listen to Jesus Christ.

United Church Observer, July 2017

WE PRAY FOR Christian unity, but in all honesty, while hatreds have thankfully declined, separation is still a gnawing reality. I'm reminded of this each time I visit the Church of the Holy Sepulchre in the Old City of Jerusalem, regarded as the spot where Jesus Christ was crucified and buried and where the resurrection took place.

So it's particularly tragic that monks from various factions have made coming to blows over who owns the place something of, well, a bad habit.

In 2008, the police arrested two clergymen who were punching and kicking each other as part of a brawl between the Armenian and Greek Orthodox contingents in the church. Four years earlier, during an Orthodox festival, a door to the Roman Catholic chapel was left open, almost certainly by mistake. The open door was regarded as disrespectful, and a fight ensued. Yet another brawl occurred during a Palm Sunday service when a Greek monk was thrown out of the church by rival clergy. When the Israeli police arrived, they were attacked by everyone present (a rare instance of Christian unity!).

Ancient, dark, and layered in shrines and compartments, the Church of the Holy Sepulchre is nothing like a conventional church and more a building constructed piecemeal over what was originally an outdoor execution site and a tomb built into a cave. Western pilgrims tend to be shocked by the overwhelming gaudiness, the sheer confusion of the place.

But this is still the centre of Christianity, surviving in the middle of a place dominated by Islam for more than a thousand years. That it exists at all is a miracle; that it is a magnet for dispute is almost inevitable.

Six denominations control the church, and their internecine disputes can be absurd to the point of hilarity. A ladder that was put over an entrance in the eighteenth century remains there today because the sects cannot agree on who has the authority to touch it.

Some of these groups are aggressively nationalist and still fighting battles that have more to do with geopolitical struggles than with the teachings of Christ. Many evangelicals prefer to think of the Garden Tomb, in another part of the city, as the authentic place of the crucifixion. It isn't, but it looks like it should be. And what is significant, of course, is that Jesus is in neither of these places. He is risen indeed.

I prefer to recall one of my many visits to this church during the height of the 2006 war in Lebanon. I sat down next to a French Franciscan priest, and we communicated in broken English, French, and Hebrew. I asked him if he still had hope that Christians, and for that matter Muslims and Jews, could eventually find resolution and peace. "Of course," he answered. "It's why I am here, why I'm a priest and why I'm a Christian." Quite so.

iPolitics, July 15, 2019

CONSERVATIVE LEADER ANDREW Scheer is in a very difficult position.

A genuinely decent man, considered by many to be far too timid for the cut and thrust of party politics, he's a devout and orthodox Roman Catholic leading a party that is divided on socially conservative issues, hoping to govern a country that is largely progressive when it comes to life and sexuality. He treads a fine line on abortion, trying to disguise his personal and theological opposition to women's choice with all sorts of obfuscating language, and struggles to justify his repeated refusal to march in Pride parades with the flimsy excuse that it's not necessary because he and his party already support LGBTQ+ equality. In fact many in his party certainly do, but Scheer is being a little disingenuous when he allows MPS Lisa Raitt or Michelle Rempel to wave the rainbow flag. You're the party leader and the gay community is well aware of your absence.

Now comes Scheer's announcement that he wants to learn more details before he supports a federal proposal to ban what is known as gay conversion therapy. The Liberal government wrote last month to the provinces and territories asking them to stop the discredited and dangerous "therapy" and they want to use the Criminal Code to make it impossible or illegal. In that an international consensus of experts and doctors — as well as politicians from most stripes — agree with this approach, Scheer's reluctance to support the government roared his ambivalence.

When I was writing my last book, *Epiphany*, I interviewed a number of men and women who had undergone various forms of conversion theory, and there are perhaps as many as twenty thousand in Canada alone. All of those who I spoke to were still gay, of course, some of them still suffering trauma because of what they had gone through. One tried to take his own life and almost succeeded.

"What you have to realize," said Gerry, who is now happily married to his long-time partner, "is that they call this a therapy to give it a varnish of medical respectability. But there is nothing medical or scientific about it. The premise of it all is that you are broken, wrong, ill, need help, have to be fixed. Imagine being told that. Imagine what that does to you."

There are various forms of this alleged therapy, but they are all based on the premise that homosexuality is undesirable, a product of nurture rather than nature and that people can be "cured." The implication is obvious, and runs against all that Canada embraces scientifically, morally and politically. Yet Andrew Scheer argues that he needs more time and more details before he comes to a decision. That simply doesn't make sense.

The spin machine went into action only hours after the Leader of the Opposition's position became clear last week. This had nothing to do with opposing equal marriage, this was not a product of homophobia, if elected the Conservatives would never dream of reopening the marriage debate and so on. Frankly I don't think a Conservative government would reopen the discussion because the country has moved on, Toronto and Quebec in particular would be aghast and even a large part of Scheer's party and caucus would be outraged. But that doesn't mean that back-benchers wouldn't be allowed to try to initiate a new debate.

There is still a vocal and powerful social conservative bloc within the Conservative party in Ottawa and even more so within the rural and suburban rank-and-file. It was these people who enabled Scheer to defeat Maxime Bernier, just as they pushed Doug Ford past Christine Elliot in Ontario. They probably have a hold of fifteen percent of the membership, and punch well above their weight.

Then there is Scheer himself. The son of a Roman Catholic deacon, he is a committed and conservative believer and like Jason Kenney is on the right of the Church. The catechism of that institution teaches that, "homosexual acts" are "intrinsically immoral and contrary to the natural law," and that even such tendencies are "objectively disordered." In other words, those in same-sex relationships are immoral and unnatural and even those who are gay but celibate are disordered. It's an ugly and jarring language, and while Canada holds to an informal separation of church and state, if a politician's faith is directly influencing his politics, surely the electorate has a right to know what he believes.

Justin Trudeau is also a Catholic, of course, as was his father and several other prime ministers, but far more on the progressive wing of the Church and, in Justin Trudeau's case, obviously a major supporter of the LGBTQ+ community. Andrew Scheer has been given several opportunities to silence his critics on these issues and to show that LGBTQ+ Canadians have nothing to fear from his becoming prime minister. Once again, however, he has failed the test, and in spite of his champions rushing to his defence, the repeated pattern is leaving a mark.

Catholic Concerns

Maclean's, December 13, 2018

POPE FRANCIS HAS the most extraordinary ability to say and write things that his supporters and staff then have to explain away, justify, obfuscate, or even downright deny. In a new book, *The Strength of a Vocation*, based on an extended interview with Spanish priest Fr. Fernando Prado, he has said that homosexuality in the priesthood is "something that worries me" and a "very serious" question. He also insists that gay priests who cannot maintain their vows of celibacy should leave the priesthood rather than live "double lives," and recommends that gay men not be allowed to enter seminaries if their homosexuality is "deep seated." He goes on to describe homosexuality as being "fashionable," and that this notion has now entered the Roman Catholic culture.

It is genuinely difficult to know where to begin. The most obvious point is that all Roman Catholic priests are supposed to be celibate, whatever their sexuality, and at first glance it's bewildering that the pontiff would single out only gay men. The reality, however, is that while the Church states in its catechism that "homosexual acts as acts of grave depravity" are "contrary to natural law," and that "homosexual acts are intrinsically disordered," most credible studies of the subject have concluded that between a quarter and half of all Roman Catholic clergy are gay. In the 2000 book *The Changing Face of the Priesthood*, for example, Father Donald Cozzens estimates that as many as fifty-eight percent of priests are gay, and that percentages are even higher for younger priests. It's impossible to be certain of course, but the caring professions have long attracted gay men, and the priesthood also enables them to avoid questions about why they are not married. Many of them are celibate, many not. How ironic that the most homophobic organization in the world should be the greatest employer of gay men!

This has all been a fairly open secret for a long time, but with the hideous revelations in the last few years about the depth and nature of the sexual abuse crisis, the Church has looked for scapegoats. In August, Bishop Robert Morlino wrote to Catholics in the Diocese of Madison, Wisconsin that, "It is time to admit that there is a homosexual subculture within the hierarchy of the Catholic Church that is wreaking great devastation in the vineyard of the Lord," and spoke of "deviant sexual — almost exclusively homosexual — acts by clerics." He received criticism but also enormous support in the Church.

In fact, the 2011 John Jay College of Criminal Justice study, commissioned by the U.S. Conference of Catholic Bishops, investigated church abuse and concluded that there was no connection between homosexuality and pedophilia, which is precisely what every other credible study has found. Francis himself has vacillated on the subject, as he has on several others. Sometimes he appears to be progressive, on other occasions, reactionary. Under this Pope, for example, it's been more difficult for a celibate gay man to enter a seminary than it was under his more conservative predecessors. The reason is that he has reissued and re-emphasized an earlier document, one that was often ignored, demanding that potential seminarians declare their sexuality, and admit if they'd had any form of same-sex attraction in recent years.

Now come these statements. The idea that homosexuality is "fashionable" is in some ways flippant, in others positively grotesque. Brazil has just elected as president a man with violently homophobic views, gay men and women are beaten and even murdered in parts of Africa, the Caribbean, and Russia and Eastern Europe. In 2016, forty-nine people were killed and fifty-three wounded in a terrorist attack inside Pulse, a gay nightclub in Orlando, Florida, and anti-gay hatred is still alive and well in North America and Europe.

Yet the leader of more than a billion Catholics thinks otherwise, and that men with "deep seated" homosexuality, even if they are sworn to celibacy, should be banned from Catholic seminaries. What Francis means by "deep seated" is unclear and one can only assume that he thinks that people can pick and choose their orientation, or be gay or straight on a part-time basis. Either way, it's shockingly banal. I was a Roman Catholic for many years, and wrote three internationally best-selling books about the Church — I can assure His Holiness that there are numerous men with "deep seated" homosexuality closer to him than he might think.

Nearer to home, I know a young gay man in Canada who sacrificed a great deal by leaving his partner and embracing celibacy. He feels called to the Roman Catholic priesthood, but has already been rejected by one seminary because they asked him several times if he was gay, and whether he had experienced same-sex attraction within the last few years. He couldn't lie. He's now looking around the world for seminaries that will simply not ask such questions, even though Rome has told them to do so. He thinks he has found one. Thus is the absurd cat-and-mouse game that is being played.

It's also a crass, gross misunderstanding of sexuality and a colossal double standard. Our sexuality is not defined and confined by our genitalia and what we do or do not do physically. It's all so much more complex and profound than that. Many husband and wife couples have an extremely limited and even non-existent sex life as they age, but they're still straight. And here's the point: potential seminarians who are heterosexual and who admit, quite naturally, to sexual or romantic temptation are never turned away for such a reason.

So the nonsense continues, but this time with a more sinister and discriminatory edge. If Francis seriously wants to address abuse, he needs to ordain women, remove the need for compulsory celibacy, dismantle clericalism, and democratize the Church, not single out some very fine men for disapproval. That's an incredibly tall order, and if it does happen, will take time, prayer, and enormous effort — but then Rome wasn't built in a day, and Roman Catholicism won't be rebuilt in one either.

CBC, February 5, 2017

POPE FRANCIS IS a conundrum. From a pontiff of glorious colours of liberation and freshness, he suddenly turns into a complacent grey and a very Latin American conservative. He promises much but, it must be said, delivers little.

The world shook just a little when, during a 2013 interview, the leader of more than a billion people said that we shouldn't judge when it came to homosexuality. Could it be, would it be, was it possible? The answer was no. It appears that he wasn't actually speaking of openly gay people but those "struggling" with their sexuality, and under his regime the Vatican has made it even more difficult, if not impossible, for even celibate gay men to be admitted into the clergy.

Catholic liberals and progressives have certainly felt empowered under Francis, but when they ask themselves what this has actually meant in the parishes, churches, and pews, many admit that it's mostly holy smoke and Roman mirrors. It is true that some conservative cardinals and church leaders have been effectively exiled or dismissed, but this may be more of a sign of Francis's authoritarianism than of genuine reform. Observers on the left as well as the right have commented that reactionary Benedict was far more tolerant of dissent than liberal Francis.

Conservative Catholics may often be difficult and bewildering — I for one have felt their abuse when I left the Roman Church and publicly supported equal marriage — but without them in the past fifty years, the Roman Catholic Church would have been in enormous trouble. After the Second Vatican Council in the 1960s, the Church's numbers hemorrhaged, seminaries emptied, and teaching was eccentric. It was usually conservatives who held the line, and Francis has been telling them for almost four years that they've got it wrong, that they are superstitious and foolish and that the people they revere are Pharisees.

Indeed he dismisses those with whom he disagrees as being Pharisaic quite often, demonstrating not only a misunderstanding of who the Pharisees actually were, but the same severely judgmental strain of which he accuses his critics. (The Pharisees were, in fact, some of the most faithful and egalitarian of Jewish activists at the time of Christ; it is because they were in direct competition with the new Christian movement they are so harshly treated in the New Testament.) Just recently, when speaking of irresponsible reporting, Francis said that people "have a tendency towards the sickness of coprophagia." For those who don't own dogs, that's eating excrement. Nice.

One of the few areas where the Catholic Church has at least opened the door to allow change to come in for a chat is whether to allow divorced and remarried Catholics to receive communion.

Yet many leading clergy, including a number of cardinals and some of them close to home, have expressed concern not only at the move, but also at how it was carried out. They argue that they were not consulted, and even that canon law is being broken.

The result has been a campaign against them that is sometimes quite shocking in its cruelty and its sinister nature. Bishop Athanasius Schneider of Kazakhstan, who had experienced the Soviet persecution of organized Christianity, told an audience that the reaction to dissenting bishops, "is a proof of the climate in which we actually live in the Church right now. We live in a climate of threats and of denial of dialogue towards a specific group." He was doubtless referring to the whispering campaign concerning their character and motives, and some of them being demoted.

It is not hyperbole to say that the Roman Catholic Church is at its most divided in fifty years. Highly influential Catholic commentators question whether the Pope is speaking for Catholicism or something entirely different. Reading between the lines — and this is something none of them would say publicly — one wonders if they genuinely accept that Francis is actually a valid pontiff.

Francis is certainly acutely political and has brought harsh Argentinian ways into church debate. But while jettisoning some of the awful pomp of previous incumbents, Francis has reintroduced certain atavistic papal attitudes about power. He is also eighty years old and not in good health. When it's time to elect a new pontiff, be prepared for a fight the like of which we haven't seen in Rome in centuries. Not a hungry lion in sight, but lots of teeth and claws.

iPolitics, December 17, 2018

THE ROMAN CATHOLIC Church is in a state of transition. Pope Francis is erratic and not as progressive as some people think, but he has at least opened up room for discussion about previously no-go areas. Right-wing priests felt empowered under Popes John Paul II and Benedict XVI. Not so under the current pontiff.

Which makes it all the more surprising that Father Jerome Lavigne, the pastor at St. Patrick's Catholic Church in Calgary — and, more significant, the vicar of Catholic education for the entire diocese — is so extraordinarily outspoken and conservative. One of his jobs is to teach the Catholic faith, in particular, to work with schools, and to prepare grade five students for confirmation. Thus we could expect a certain degree of sensitivity from the man, especially regarding sexuality, which affects young people so profoundly.

Yet he's made the most incendiary comments about the LGBT+ community in homilies and writings, some of which have only recently been exposed. In the past few days, for example, a deeply homophobic essay and homily has come to light, in which Lavigne condemns "fornication, homosexual acts, prostitution, pedophilia, sodomy." He also says it's untrue that people are born gay, then attacks the rainbow flag, the symbol of the gay community. He says it was "selected to represent lawlessness, promiscuous lifestyles that are a direct break from the established order of the natural law," and that it "stands before us as a sacrilege of unfathomable proportions. This is nothing short of spitting and laughing in God's face."

Speaking of the origins of the rainbow flag, Lavigne says: "And who's the master behind all of this? It's not flesh and blood. It's way too ingenious ... There is only one who twists truth to this level. Who unleashes unfathomable proportions by means of taking that which exists as a covenant that God established, and completely turning it on its head so that it represents, once again, the very evil from which God's reprimanding hand was unleashed upon creation in the very first place? ... His name is Satan."

Satan was unavailable for comment, but when a complaint was made to the Roman Catholic diocese of Calgary, they removed the homily from Facebook and church websites, and responded: "The review of Fr. Lavigne's homily recognizes that the reading from the Book of Genesis expanded to include some reflections on homosexuality. However, these reflections did not fully capture that we are all called to live a life of chastity according to our state in life. We are all created by God and He loves us all so that each person receives from God their inherent dignity. The Catholic Church advocates for the common good of society, so that we live together in an atmosphere of peace, safety and respect for the dignity of one another regardless of age, ancestry, body image, culture, sexual orientation and religion."

Yet if this is the case, why is Lavigne still vicar for Catholic education? These are not isolated comments. He has also said: "What our Lord is making quite clear for us is that the actions we commit to doing in this life are voluntary and deliberated ... There's no such thing as 'God made me this way,' and so I can take part in 'Depraved, Intrinsically and Gravely Disordered Actions.' That's a 'self-taught lie' that serves to masquerade Evil as a great good to be experienced!"

And there is more. In 2016, he had the notorious alt-right activist Faith Goldy speak at his church on "Unmasking the Architects and Evils of Sexual Education," in which she told the audience that Ontario was in crisis and discussed former Ontario premier Kathleen Wynne's sexuality at length, claiming that Wynne had used her sexuality to "muzzle" any criticism of Ontario's sex education curriculum. "In case you guys don't know," said Goldy, "she is a lesbian."

All this has become public after a series of damning revelations regarding Alberta's Catholic church and the gay community in the province. First, high-profile Calgary Catholic lawyer John Carpay was exposed for having compared the rainbow flag to the Nazi swastika. Next, a two-decade-old speech by Alberta's United Conservative Party Leader Jason Kenney was revealed, in which he boasts of working during the height of the AIDS crisis in San Francisco on a campaign to prevent gay men in hospital from being allowed to see their partners. Then, just a few days ago, the scandal broke that Alberta Catholic school boards were allegedly not employing people in same-sex relationships, and were asking teachers to "out" their colleagues.

Removing videos and making anodyne statements simply won't do. Father Jerome Lavigne and the Roman Catholic diocese of Calgary have some explaining to do. Sin, as they surely must know, may be forgiven, but only after the culprit admits, acknowledges, and promises to change.

CBC, October 19, 2018

POPE FRANCIS HAS the most extraordinary ability to say the wrong things, often at the most sensitive times. Last Friday, he accepted the resignation of the archbishop of Washington, Cardinal Donald Wuerl — a controversial figure accused of doing too little to prevent, and perhaps even deliberately covering up, hideous sexual abuse cases.

Beyond simply accepting his resignation, Francis took the highly unusual step of releasing a public letter where he praised his friend, arguing that he had been used as a scapegoat. While he admitted that Wuerl had made some "mistakes," he said that he had acted with "nobility" and remarked that he was "proud" of him. He also asked the cardinal to continue to act as the archdiocese's apostolic administrator — in effect to remain in his position — until a successor could be named.

It's about as enthusiastic and supportive as is possible in the circumstances, concerning a man whose predecessor as archbishop, Theodore McCarrick, had to resign when he was accused of sexually abusing seminarians and minors.

Many informed commentators find it difficult to believe that Wuerl knew nothing about this before it was made public. He was also bishop of Pittsburgh from 1988 to 2006, and a recent grand jury report chronicled an entire litany of the most grotesque and widespread sexual abuse throughout Pennsylvania. Either Wuerl was spectacularly myopic and incompetent in dealing with this or, as many have suggested, he sometimes protected abusers.

What we do know, according to that grand jury report, is that in 1998 he allowed Father William O'Malley to return to a parish after numerous reports were made against him, and after his own admission that he was sexually attracted to young people. He went on to abuse again. Seven years later, Wuerl also reinstated Father George Zirwas, after several credible abuse accusations.

Wuerl did sometimes expose and expel abusers, but his record is inconsistent at best, and since the Pennsylvania report his reputation has suffered enormously. Yet his ability to evince enthusiasm for conservatives such as Benedict and relative liberals such as Francis has served him well, and he has supporters in all sorts of high places. In many ways, however, Wuerl is largely irrelevant in all this — a mere symptom of a far more systemic crisis. It was Francis himself who, until obliged to apologize, scolded abuse survivors in Chile, and accused Irish survivor and activist Marie Collins as being "fixated." As with many issues, he is erratic and changeable, but has certainly disappointed victims of Catholic clergy abuse with his inaction, and now with this public endorsement of Cardinal Wuerl.

There are currently investigations into Catholic clergy abuse in several U.S. states, including New York and Michigan, and the consensus within the Catholic media is that the findings will be similar to those in Pennsylvania. It's not certain how Pope Francis will react, but it's highly unlikely that very much will change. Church leaders are certainly more careful now, but the fundamentals and causes remain firmly in place.

There are four major problems. Enforced celibacy can lead to lies and obfuscation, and while men who are denied sex do not automatically become abusers, there's no doubt that abusers certainly look for places where they can disguise their sexual perversions and their crimes.

Second is the patriarchy that dominates within the Church. Women are not only refused ordination, but are excluded from all positions of power. Abusers in any area are overwhelmingly men, and the sheer presence of women would create a more normal and balanced culture.

Then there is authority, which is as firmly guarded by priests on the left as well as by those on the right. The Roman Catholic Church is based on hierarchy, with the Pope considered the direct successor to St. Peter, given the keys of the kingdom by Jesus Himself. Those he makes bishops, and those the bishops then make priests, are not to be contradicted. This clericalism may not be as severe as it once was, but in essence it hasn't changed.

Last is the climate of secrecy that exists, and is a direct consequence of the first three aspects of all this. The upper echelons of the Roman Catholic Church are still a closed shop, with the laity given occasional, but largely cosmetic views through the stained glass windows. So much is kept secret that abusers, who of course represent a small minority of clergy, find it relatively easy to hide.

None of this can or will be addressed until a genuinely revolutionary and courageous pope is elected, and one who is willing to turn the Church upside down and shake it into modernity and accountability. Miracles do happen I suppose, but they're very few and far between these days.

Maclean's, January 21, 2019

POPE FRANCIS IS adored by liberal Catholics and by many in the secular
world — who, frankly, know little of what he actually believes — he is
regarded by church conservatives, including some clergy, as irresponsible
and even heretical. The truth is that while he is progressive on issues of
ecology, immigration, and economics, he has been extremely slow to
react to abuse issues, and just last week was accused of being aware that
a close friend, Bishop Gustavo Zanchetta, was known to have taken
naked selfies and indulged in obscene behaviour. He accepted the man's
resignation in August 2017, but it is claimed that he knew of his fellow
Argentinian's actions two years earlier, and rather than punish the man,
appointed him to a senior Vatican position.

When charges such as this are made public, the Pope and his people
tend to try to digress and distract. Which may have something to do
with his new announcement of an app to encourage the world's billion
Roman Catholics to pray. Called rather glibly "Click to Pray," the app
tells users what Francis is praying for, and they can then click the thing
and join the person regarded by Catholics as the direct descendant of
St. Peter, in holy and devout prayer. At the app's launch in Rome, Francis

was apparently praying about disaster. "Today, I have two pains in my heart. Colombia and the Mediterranean." The first referred to a car bombing, the second to the drowning of 170 migrants. Both events being deeply disturbing and serious. Francis emphasized the app is so he can "stay in touch with others, to share values and projects and to express the desire to form a community." Well, that's okay then.

It's a little difficult not to be cynical about this apparent embrace of the modern and the ostensibly relevant when Francis rules over a church that still forbids contraception, women's choice, and female ordination, is mired in patriarchy and wealth, and under his pontificate — contrary to what people believe — gay men, even if they are celibate, have been told that they are not wanted in the priesthood and that they live in a state of "objective disorder."

And what is the man saying about the nature of prayer? It's not the stuff of gimmicks, and one of my main concerns as a Christian is that prayer is abused and exploited both as a word and a concept. Politicians obsessively tell us that they are praying when a tragedy occurs, and public figures who have never prayed in their lives send their "thoughts and prayers." Prayer is not an emotional spasm, not an empty gesture, not a substitute for action. For the Christian, and for most people of faith, it's a dialogue with God, an expression of a relationship, a conversation and a conduit. Søren Kierkegaard put it like this: "Just as in earthly life lovers long for the moment when they are able to breathe forth their love for each other, to let their souls blend in a soft whisper, so the mystic longs for the moment when in prayer he can, as it were, creep into God."

I pray silently, pray formally during set offices, pray even in stressful public situations when I feel slightly awkward doing so. I could no more not pray than not eat, and rather like food, prayer often delights me, sometimes leaves me disappointed, but always nourishes me. But prayer should not be watered down until it seems meaningless and banal, rather like a handshake or a casual "How are you?" Prayer is about letting go, allowing, accepting. In a way, it's a profound acquiescence, a sometimes reluctant acceptance that we may not know what is best and that there is someone above and beyond us. That's why prayer is so important. It helps us find the prism of faith and filter of intellect through which we can understand the meaning of texts written so long ago.

Which is why the notion of a prayer app is so jarring, especially when it comes from the Pope! It's almost reminiscent of the selling of indulgences by the Roman Catholic Church in the early sixteenth century, one of the events that led to the Reformation. It all seems so robotic, formal, artificial and — forgive me — irreligious. At a time when hardly a week goes by without another disgusting revelation concerning priests sexually abusing children and the Church doing nothing about it and often disguising or denying the crimes, this surely cannot be the most appropriate and ethical use of the Pope's time and influence. Beware fiddling while Rome burns, whether you're a Caesar or a Pope. I will pray for Francis over all this; but not by using his app.

iPolitics, April 17, 2018

POPES HAVE BECOME rather good at apologizing in recent years. Actually, they've had no option. The clergy abuse crisis, the historic persecution and slaughter of heretics, the Vatican's ambivalence towards Nazi anti-Semitism during the Second World War, and so many other horrific events all have demanded public contrition. Pope Francis has a mixed record on the subject: he can be progressive and enlightened in some areas, tribal and reactionary in others. Recently in Chile, for example he initially caused outrage by not only refusing to apologize for clerical abuse, but for lambasting some of its victims. He later reversed his position, largely due to public fury.

Now we come to Canada, and the ghastly case of residential schools, and the treatment of Indigenous people. No particular denomination or institution — secular or religious — is solely to blame, and government is as guilty as church, but most have made seemingly heartfelt apologies. Stephen Harper, Justin Trudeau, the Anglican Church, the Presbyterian Church. The same was asked of Pope Francis, speaking for Canada's Roman Catholics, especially as they are the largest Christian group in the country. The response, alas, was in the negative.

Now, Parliament intends to formally ask the Pope to reconsider his refusal to apologize, and for the Church to fulfil its financial obligations under the Indian Residential Schools Settlement Agreement. This was initiated by NDP MP Charlie Angus, and backed, with edits, by Carolyn Bennett, the Minister of Crown-Indigenous Relations. It asks the Church to raise twenty-five million dollars for Indigenous healing, as demanded in the residential schools settlement of 2007, and to supply relevant documents that could help reconciliation.

A papal apology was one of the ninety-four recommendations from the Truth and Reconciliation Commission, and to emphasize the importance of the gesture, when he visited the Vatican last year, Justin Trudeau personally asked the Pope to consider the apology. Such a direct request is considered extremely significant in Rome.

Even so, the official response was that while the Pope takes all this "seriously" (well, that's nice to know), "after carefully considering the request and extensive dialogue with the bishops of Canada, he felt that he could not personally respond."

As that statement makes clear, the Pope didn't make this decision alone, and for that matter it's not even clear that he made the decision at all. His representatives in Canada, including senior bishops and cardinals, and likely lawyers, would have made suggestions, and it's uncommon for Rome to contradict such advice.

If change is going to happen, it will require pressure and exposure. It took many years for Rome to admit, acknowledge, and then apologize for generations of sexual abuse of countless children, and it only did so after denial, obfuscation, and even emotional and legal attacks on those who had been so appallingly treated by its clergy. The Church has learned how to play the long game, and to cover itself in case of litigation.

In 1991, for example, the Canadian Catholic Bishops issued a statement that "We are sorry and deeply regret the pain, suffering and alienation that so many experienced" at the residential schools, and two years later said that, "various types of abuse experienced at some residential schools have moved us to a profound examination of conscience as a Church." But these are couched and careful words, obviously written through the filter of lawyers rather than the heart of conscience.

When asked his opinion, Andrew Scheer, a devout Roman Catholic who knows Catholic leaders well, responded that "all religions" involved in the residential school system should admit what happened. Presumably he was trying to draw equivalents, and protect Catholicism from being singled out. Problem is, the only thing that distinguishes the Roman Catholic Church is that it's about the only faith not to have issued an absolute apology from its highest point of leadership!

In 1986, the United Church made an official statement that spoke volumes: "We imposed our civilization as a condition of accepting the gospel. We tried to make you be like us and in so doing we helped to destroy the vision that made you what you were. As a result, you, and we, are poorer and the image of the Creator in us is twisted, blurred, and we are not what we are meant by God to be. We ask you to forgive us and to walk together with us in the Spirit of Christ so that our peoples may be blessed and God's creation healed."

The Roman Catholic Church may argue that it's sufficient for a local diocese or organization to apologize, and that a papal statement is unnecessary. That just won't do. Indigenous people, the victims, have asked for this apology, explaining how much it will heal their wounds. Good Lord, the truth cries out to be heard. The Gospel of Matthew says, "So when you are offering your gift at the altar, if you remember that your brother or sister has something against you, leave your gift there before the altar and go; first be reconciled to your brother or sister, and then come and offer your gift." In other words, no Christian can go forward unless they apologize for the wrong and the crime that they've committed. That applies to all Christians, even to Popes.

The Walrus, September 6, 2017

ANYBODY WHO KEEPS an eye on Roman Catholic politics would not have been at all surprised by a recent article in *La Civilta Cattolica*, a Jesuit journal published in Rome which carries the Holy See's stamp of approval. What appears in its pages, in other words, is supported by Pope Francis. The most recent issue carried a scathing attack on Catholic conservatives in the United States, condemning them for forming an axis of "hate" with evangelical Christians to elect and support President Donald Trump. The piece names Steve Bannon, Trump's former advisor, as a "supporter of apocalyptic geopolitics" and speaks of the Catholic right's denial of climate change and opposition to immigration. The article pulls no clerical punches, even going so far as to juxtapose the theology of the U.S. Catholic right with jihadism.

The article doesn't reference Canada directly, but there's plenty of evidence that right-wing Catholics are helping harden Canada's conservative party and exerting more political influence than Canadians would like to think. To grasp why this is happening begins with understanding the Catholic Church's current state in North America. The institution is divided in three distinct ways. First are the Catholic hierarchies. They tend to be relatively thoughtful and moderate. Second comes the laity. Most are indifferent, and even those who are regular Communicants generally embrace the culture around them rather than the teaching of their church. On issues of contraception and equal marriage, for example, they are as progressive as non-Catholics.

Third, however, are Roman Catholic activists. They collect around the abortion issue, seen as the great litmus test for orthodoxy and taking up most of the time and energy of the Catholic right. Added to this is a resistance to LGBT+ equality, assisted dying, anything seen as permissive or pornographic, and hence any form of liberalism. That invariably slides into greater conservatism, on economic as well as social and religious issues. These activists are a minority, but they are well financed and dedicated. In 2010, for example, the Ontario Premier Dalton McGuinty felt obliged to withdraw a long-overdue reform of the sex education curriculum after various parental and activist groups — with a strong Catholic conservative base — mobilized in opposition. They took out ads, held demonstrations, threatened to unseat Liberal politicians, and promised the mass withdrawal of children from schools. The campaign worked.

What applies to the U.S. also applies to Canada. Remember that the two most prominent conservatives in Canada — Jason Kenney and Andrew Scheer — are right-wing Catholics. Kenney has attended meetings of the conservative group Opus Dei, an ultra-Catholic organization that tries to recruit people prominent in business and finance. Scheer is a committed believer and the son of a deacon — an ordained position for men considered only slightly junior to that of priest. While the new leader of the opposition may smile a great deal and claim that he will not reopen debates about abortion and gay rights, his personal views on these issues are absolute. It's interesting that Stephen Harper was long considered a social conservative and a right-wing Christian, given that he was often hostile to Christian activists in his caucus who wanted to resurrect social and moral issues. The same cannot be said for Andrew Scheer, who has already spoken of removing funding from universities where "free speech" is not protected; this is a euphemism for the protection of anti-abortion groups who now routinely demand the right on campus to present graphic images of aborted fetuses.

The leadership is one thing but what also sent shockwaves through the Conservative Party was the success of the other, even more obvious and hardline Catholic candidate Pierre Lemieux in the recent leadership contest. As the *Toronto Star* reported back in May, "In six Scarborough ridings, either of two social conservative candidates, Brad Trost or Pierre Lemieux, was the first choice of between twenty and fifty-five percent of Conservative members." This sort of thing doesn't go unnoticed inside the party, and while it frightens social liberals it delights their opponents and makes pragmatists — those who simply want to win at any cost — begin to wonder about future policy.

This in turn flows over to the think tanks. Cardus is probably the most senior, describing its mission as being "the renewal of North American social architecture" — very much conservative shorthand. It brings together religious activists, mainly from the Catholic and evangelical right. It produces various publications, including Convivium, and its annual lecture series funded by the Hill Companies has featured Rex Murphy, Barbara Kay, and Conrad Black.

Far more intense is the virulently anti-abortion and anti-LGBT+ outfit Campaign Life Coalition and the website Lifesite News. This online media entity is overwhelmingly Catholic and undeniably influential. When Ontario's youngest and arguably most conservative MPP Sam Oosterhoff won the Tory nomination for Niagara West, party organizers from Toronto complained that "those Campaign Life people were bloody everywhere." His victory stunned the party establishment.

Lifesite recently ran an article describing Donald Trump as the new Constantine, the Roman emperor who gave Christianity his official blessing. It has claimed that, "The entire world owes a debt of gratitude to the president" and has described Trump's opponents as "satanic." The site has endless references to sinister cabals, the influence of various behind-the-scenes controllers, and the usual dark conspiracy theories. In February, for example, it argued that the opposition to Trump was orchestrated and funded by "the several decades-old movement for an aggressively secular, borderless, de-populationist New World Order and world government."

Thing is, Lifesite is not a blog that's read only by its writers. It's a massively well-financed platform consumed by hundreds of thousands of people, many if not most of them in Canada. Much of the money is given by devoted followers, with special appeals whenever money is short or a particular campaign is being planned.

Even more blatant than Lifesite are blogs such as the Ontario-based Vox Cantoris and Toronto Catholic Witness, with less significance but still making a heavy mark. The latter wrote this, shortly after the terrible massacre at the Ariana Grande concert in which twenty-two people were killed and more than one hundred injured, many of them children:

"A few minutes on the internet this morning identified her as a promoter of sexual libertinism, pornography, obscenity, profanity, feminism, and the LGBTQ agenda. Yet for all of this, it seems that parents have no qualms about sending their pre-teen and teen girls to listen and watch this loathsome individual ... I cannot but be puzzled how parents who seemingly are so distressed about the killing of their children, but remained utterly unconcerned that their children were slowly being spiritually poisoned."

Anybody who has been on the receiving end of right-wing Canadian Catholic zealots knows, alas, that such a tone is by no means unique. When I left the Roman Catholic Church and began to champion progressive causes, I was accused of being an adulterer, a thief, and even a pedophile. My wife was told to leave me, my children's Facebook pages were trolled, and there were successful campaigns to have me fired from speeches and columns.

That tone is also starting to shape the public discourse around issues. At this precise time, for instance, there is a struggle taking place at St. Michael's, the Catholic college at the University of Toronto. On the one side are conservative Catholics who want to restore the Catholicity of the college, on the other a more liberal group who are influenced by the Pope Francis approach and look to influence others by witness rather than muscular certainty. The story has already made the national media — highly unusual for religious news.

In many ways, it's a battle for the soul and future of the Catholic Church in Canada. Who controls this major Catholic college at the most important university in Canada — the bishops and cardinal or liberal clergy and lay academics? It's not irrelevant that immediately after this story became public, the blog Toronto Catholic Witness ran a long entry defending the right-wing at St. Michael's and accusing the college of being home to lewd sexual behaviour.

St. Michael's educates many of the most prominent politicians and social and economic leaders who are nominally Catholic. If the orthodox voices win this noisy and increasingly acrimonious argument, we may see a much more rigid and religious formation of the future Catholic elite. It's ironic that as the Vatican moves to embrace more liberal positions, the Canadian church looks in the opposite direction. Are we witnessing a historic and momentous Canadian moment? Perhaps. But don't expect a CBC montage.

The Globe and Mail, February 26, 2019

THEY CAME, THEY spoke, they left — and nothing changed. Pope Francis and 190 prelates gathered last Thursday for an unprecedented 4 day summit in Rome to discuss the Church's sexual abuse crisis, and the result is very much business as usual. Nothing had been guaranteed, but the sheer optics of the event implied that something, at long last, might be done to respond to a circus of horrors that unwraps by the week.

Instead, the Pope refused to enact the anticipated "zero tolerance" when dealing with pedophile priests, delivering instead a platitude that the Church would "spare no effort" — sound that signified nothing.

To make matters worse, he then devoted a large part of his concluding speech to the subject of sexual abuse in general society, arguing that it's not confined to the Roman Catholic Church and that most offenders were family members, "husbands of child brides and teachers."

"Our work has made us realize once again that the gravity of the scourge of the sexual abuse of minors is, and historically has been, a widespread phenomenon in all cultures and societies," he continued. "I am reminded of the cruel religious practice, once widespread in certain cultures, of sacrificing human beings — frequently children — in pagan rites."

The degree of digression here is incredible. Nobody has ever claimed that the Church is the only offender, but that it has denied and obfuscated, protected its own, and even attacked victims who spoke out for justice. The phenomenon of child marriage is something entirely different; that human sacrifice was even mentioned is bewildering. This is what is known as "Rome speak," where much is said and little admitted.

Abuse, tragically, exists everywhere there is a power dynamic, and that includes families, schools, sports clubs and other religious institutions. But the Church continues to refuse to examine why it is especially vulnerable, and even under the allegedly progressive Pope Francis, it still cannot acknowledge the depth and extent of the problem. In spite of papal protests, the Roman Catholic Church remains a magnet for this kind of crime, and nothing will change without reckoning with and resolving five basic aspects that in some ways are built into the religion's bones: Enforced celibacy, patriarchy, clericalism, secrecy, and sexual dishonesty.

Celibacy does not lead to abuse, and if it's voluntary, it can be deeply spiritual. But when it's demanded, it can attract the sexually immature and broken, and can enforce a dark stigma around sexuality. Patriarchy within Roman Catholicism is staggeringly obvious — the image of almost 200 middle-aged and elderly men discussing sexual abuse surely says it all. Women perpetrate abuse too, of course, but a culture so lacking in gender balance and female influence can never function healthily.

Clericalism and secrecy run together, with the priest — he who stands for Jesus Christ during the Mass — still considered part of the elite. Father can do no wrong, the child claiming abuse has to be lying, and the Church must guard its internal life from those who would criticize and question.

Sexual dishonesty? The number of Catholic priests who are gay is high, with estimates ranging between thirty to seventy percent. Gay men are no more likely to abuse than straight men, but they are forced to live a lie within a Church that is still deeply homophobic. That cloud of dishonesty is exploited by abusers.

Yes, the meeting did produce an eight-point pledge promising more transparency, less defensiveness and an insistence on clergy purity — but this is mere rhetoric. The inescapable fact is that myriad complaints concerning child rape have been made for decades, and the Church has consistently refused to help the victim, deal with the abuser and look at the root causes. It only began to deal with these obscenities when it was forced to do so by media and legal exposure.

So in that context, the gathered flock's failure to enact real change is particularly damning. They could have vowed to ordain women and openly gay men, encourage the equality of all believers, and open up the doors and the books. But it was never going to happen, and likely never will happen in our lifetimes. Further monstrosities will come to light, and more empty gestures will be offered. I wish I could be more optimistic, but I know the Church too well — and how reluctant it has long been to accepting radical change and in trying to genuinely transform the comfortable status quo.

The Walrus, May 13, 2015

BACK IN 1999, British author John Cornwell published a controversial and widely publicized book called *Hitler's Pope: The Secret History of Pius XII*. The title was misleading on two levels: first, in that it implied and depicted Pius as a faithful Nazi; second, in that it assumed the man's story long had been kept a secret. Six years later came a counter-blast in the shape of *The Myth of Hitler's Pope: How Pope Pius XII Rescued Jews from the Nazis* by David G. Dalin, who is not only Jewish, but also a rabbi.

So there we had it. A liberal Catholic accusing a pope of Nazism; a Jewish academic and ordained cleric praising the wartime pontiff as a friend of anti-Nazism and the Jewish people. The twenty-first-century Pius wars had begun. And now, another front has opened, with the making by Catholic director and writer Liana Marabini of a movie called *Shades of Truth*, which will be shown at this month's Cannes Film Festival. It's extremely supportive of Pope Pius, presenting a man who utters progressive aphorisms as he strides along Vatican hallways shaming his contemporaries as they fail to properly empathize with Europe's poor Jews. It also makes the outlandish claim that Pius saved

800,000 Jewish lives, a boast that even his most aggressive academic supporters would never make.

In one scene, which naturally is used in marketing materials for the film, Pius is shown wearing a yellow star pinned to his papal cassock. It never happened in real life, of course; and even in *Shades of Truth*, the scene is confined to a dream sequence. So it's misleading at best, if not noisily dishonest.

But imagine if the leader of world Catholicism really had worn such a symbol of degradation and genocide? Urban legend long has had it that the King of Denmark wore such a star as he rode the streets of Copenhagen in his carriage; it's not true, but the point is that those who knew him always accepted the anecdote because it was authentic to his character and attitude toward his Jewish subjects. The King of Morocco actually did request yellow stars for himself and his family when told that Moroccan Jews would have to wear them. And this from an Arab Muslim monarch living under occupation. But with Pius, the story simply doesn't fit. Even in dream.

The story of Eugenio Pacelli, elected to the papacy in March 1939 as Pius XII, is complex. Anyone searching for absolute purity of motive and some sort of anachronistic philo-semitism and embrace of modern pluralism will be disappointed. He was a man of his time and his faith: obsessively frightened of Communism and its campaign against the Church; obviously unaware of who would triumph in the Second World War. His official actions consistently reflected these fears and uncertainties.

Pius XII almost certainly had no personal animus against Jewish people, always rejected the eugenics and intolerance of National Socialism, and on a personal level did what he could to save the lives of Jews around him. Before he became Pope, Cardinal Pacelli drafted the papal encyclical condemning Nazi racism and had it read from every pulpit. As Pope, he had the Vatican use its assets to ransom Jews from the Nazis, ran an elaborate escape route, and hid Jewish families in the papal palace of Castel Gondolfo. In 1945, Rabbi Herzog of Jerusalem, for example, thanked Pius, "for his lifesaving efforts on behalf of the Jews during the occupation of Italy." When the pontiff died in 1958, Golda Meir, then Israeli foreign minister, delivered a eulogy at the United Nations praising the man for his work on behalf of her people.

For almost a generation, in fact, it was considered a political absolute that the Church was a member of a coalition of victims during the Second World War, and Pius was mentioned alongside Churchill and Roosevelt as part of the team of morally correct wartime leaders. It was only in the 1960s that the conversation around this issue began to change, partly because of the work of a German playwright named Rolf Hochhuth, who alleged in his 1963 play *The Deputy* that the Vatican not only had ignored the suffering of the Jews, but tacitly and some-times explicitly had supported the Nazis. The truth, however, is more of a via media than a via dolorosa.

While the Pope did not issue an outright attack on the Nazis' treat-ment of the Jews, his supporters argue that this was because the leaders of the Catholic Church in Holland had made just such a public state-ment condemning the Nazi deportation of the Jewish people. In response the Germans had arrested and murdered every Dutch Jewish convert to Catholicism they could find. (Tragically, those arrests and deportations were only a matter of time anyway.)

Pius was such a friend of the Jews, the argument continues, that when the Chief Rabbi of Rome, Israel Zolli, converted to Roman Catholicism after the war, he took Pius's name, Eugenio, in his christen-ing as a tribute to the Pope's work on behalf of the Jews. That's also true but doesn't really change much. On a personal level, as noted above, Pius certainly did what he could to save lives; but on a public level — where multitudes could be saved — he did far less.

Pius was not "Hitler's Pope," and the Nazis always considered him a threat. His failure was that he never made that threat a reality by speaking out resolutely against the Holocaust, invariably terrified of what would happen to the world's Catholics if he did and advised by some around him that the alternative to the Germans was the Soviets. It's an understandable dilemma, but a defiant Pope could have influenced hundreds of millions of Catholics, many of them serving in armies allied to the Germans. The risk would have been enormous, but Christianity isn't supposed to be about safety and complacency.

Thus there are indeed numerous shades of truth around Pope Pius. Unfortunately, this movie only deepens the polarization and so makes it more difficult for a reasonable analysis to take place. The late Sir Martin Gilbert, one of the finest historians of the Holocaust and the Second World War and a man I was fortunate enough to call a friend, once put it like this: "This was a pre-Vatican II Catholic Church in the middle of a war that, for the most part, was not between Germans and the west, but Nazis and Stalinists. If, say, John Paul II had been Pope, the story may have been different. Throw in subsequent rifts between the Catholic right and left, and the regrettable politicization of the Shoah and truth is extremely difficult to find."

The entire political and religious landscape has changed today, and some of these old battles obscure contemporary truths. Pius didn't act particularly badly for a man of his era but, I suppose, he did act particularly normally. For someone thought to be the direct successor to St. Peter, given the keys of the kingdom by Jesus Christ, that's just not good enough, no matter how well that truth is shaded.

Toronto Star, July 10, 2019

EARLIER THIS YEAR I had the misfortune of going to see the contro-versial anti-abortion movie *Unplanned*. In full disclosure, I didn't go for a night's entertainment but as a journalistic exercise.

The movie is appalling. The acting is so wooden as to be amusing, the plot is cliché upon caricature, the depiction of abortion-providers is cartoonish, and it's all wrapped up in gory and ghoulish scenes of the blood-soaked hands of evil liberals and snarling feminists.

It's partly financed by a pillow-manufacturer named Mike Lindell, who once said that Donald Trump was "the greatest president in history ... chosen by God." A pillow would have helped me when I watched, but not those around me. People were engaged! They cried, screamed, and prayed. There was palpable anger, and a cheering and clapping when the movie ended.

That reaction is pertinent, because abortion medics have been attacked and killed, and anti-abortion extremists are considered a domestic ter-rorist threat in the U.S. And there is no doubt that while it's raw, clumsy, and didactic, the ranting of *Unplanned* does succeed in creating an atmosphere of fear and anger, and that can have terrible consequences.

The story concerns anti-abortion activist Abby Johnson, on whose memoir the movie is based. Many medical experts question the book and the film, but testimony from doctors has never been an obstacle for the anti-abortion movement.

In this story, Abby glides from being a supporter of choice and a clinic worker to a fierce opponent of abortion. It's all about profit and money, the movie insists, and even if it wasn't, a fetus can feel pain. Let's just hope then that no unborn child has to sit through this agonizing nonsense.

MY FIRST JOB in journalism was at the *New Statesman* magazine in Britain in the early 1980s. I was new and shiny and one of the first people I met was a man who was not new and shone in an entirely different way. Christopher Hitchens — he didn't like "Chris" — was as generous as he was gifted. But he didn't suffer fools or frauds.

One of the most famous of the latter was, in his opinion, a woman who is about to be acknowledged as a saint by the Roman Catholic Church. Mother Teresa, born in Skopje, now Macedonia, to Albanian parents, as Anjezë Gonxhe Bojaxhiu, and someone whom to many embodies the best in Christianity. Hitchens disagreed, wrote a book about her called *The Missionary Position* and insisted that she was a force for evil rather than good.

I would not be as bold, and could not be as brilliant, as the exquisite Hitch but Good God — and I do believe Him to be good and great — he had a point. Hitchens' argument, among others, was that Mother Teresa provided sub-standard medical care, took money from dictators and criminals and often cozied up to them, pushed her faith on the vulnerable and sick, and encouraged western Catholic journalists to paint her as divine.

There are indeed many unanswered questions about the level of aid the poor of Calcutta actually received and it's beyond dispute that Teresa was heavily funded by brutes such as Jean-Claude Duvalier of Haiti, who stole a fortune from his own people while they lived in poverty. Not only did she take the man's cash, she lionized him as a great leader. She also praised the repugnant Albanian despot Enver Hoxha and laid flowers at his grave and welcomed donations from British publisher and criminal Robert Maxwell.

The case of the anti-pornography zealot and businessman Charles Keating is particularly disturbing. He gave millions of dollars to Teresa and the use of his private jet when she visited the United States. Although he was sent to prison for more than four years for fraud, and thousands of people were hurt by what he did, Teresa refused to refund any of the money he had donated.

There are also ideological and systemic problems. She campaigned against contraceptive use in a country ravaged by over-population and it almost goes without saying that she vehemently opposed abortion rights. Her motivation was conservative Catholic rather than progressively human. "I think it is very beautiful for the poor to accept their lot, to share it with the passion of Christ," she said. "I think the world is being much helped by the suffering of the poor people." That is not how the poor feel as they watch their babies die in their arms.

It's important to emphasize that there are countless Catholic and other Christian groups performing outstanding work in India and elsewhere who do not adopt Teresa's reactionary views and dubious ways, and do not have or want the public relations machine that she enjoyed. Some of the most successful social programs in India are funded internationally by western governments who also urge family planning, LGBT+ equality and divorce rights, all opposed not only by the new saint, but by her church. More than this, the bulk of the good and selfless work being performed in India is by Indian Hindus and Muslims, not white Christians.

The ceremony announcing to the world that Mother Teresa can be prayed to and revered will take place in a Vatican in possession of wealth through paintings, manuscripts, statues and investments that is beyond comprehension, and in spite of a few utterly cosmetic changes by Pope Francis there is no indication that this will ever change. The glaring juxtaposition between what the tiny Albanian woman was at least supposed to represent and the Roman reality is, frankly, scandalous.

It was another Catholic, the Brazilian archbishop Dom Helder Camara, who said, "When I give food to the poor, they call me a saint. When I ask why the poor have no food, they call me a communist." But he and his liberation theology were not popular with a Papacy that embraced a woman who refused to ask the right questions, apologized for the culprits and ignored the causes.

Maclean's, August 3, 2018

IN ARGUABLY THE most dramatic move of his five-year pontificate, Pope Francis has declared that the death penalty is wrong in all circumstances, arguing that capital punishment is "an attack on the inviolability and dignity of the person," and that the Church will campaign "with determination" for the universal abolition of executions. Popes John Paul II and Benedict XVI had made their opposition clear, but this represents an evolution of the official teaching — that it was acceptable if it was "the only practicable way" to save lives — which gave plenty of wiggle room for interpretation. Now, however, Francis hasn't just solidified the teaching, but he has placed it in the Catechism of the Roman Catholic Church, the doctrinal guide to the faith that is central to international Catholicism. It has, as it were, biblical prestige.

But there will, of course, be opponents to this bold shift. Indeed, when Francis deployed the phrase "dignity of the person," it was loaded: it was also used by the Church in its opposition to abortion and assisted dying, and indeed the chapter in the catechism that deals with capital punishment also outlines Catholic teaching regarding these two issues. The proximity will escape neither supporters nor opponents.

Indeed, it's largely because of powerful opposition that Francis's predecessors were reluctant to go any further than their personal opposition, partly because they knew how many lay members of their church disagreed with them — particularly Catholic politicians in the United States, where capital punishment is legal in thirty-one American states and also at the federal level. Governors Greg Abbott of Texas and Pete Ricketts of Nebraska, for example, are Catholics who proclaim their faith politically as well as personally; both have presided over executions. The late Justice Antonin Scalia, the doyen of Catholic lawyers, wrote that, "I do not find the death penalty immoral." President Donald Trump's Supreme Court nominee Brett M. Kavanaugh is a Catholic, as are Chief Justice John G. Roberts Jr. and Justices Clarence Thomas, Samuel A. Alito Jr. and Sonia Sotomayor. They will likely respond just as Paul Martin and Justin Trudeau do over issues such as abortion and equal marriage: *We are Catholics, but we govern for all of the country, and must separate church and state.* It may be a messy separation to make.

But this all goes much deeper than the formalization of a view long held in the Vatican, and is more part of the continuum of a reforming Pope who, at eighty-one and in questionable health, wants to leave a mark than cannot be erased. Francis is beloved by media, juxtaposed as he sometimes is with Trump's crass, right-wing populism, and he has made laudable statements about climate change, economic equality, and social reform. But in truth, very little has changed in Rome. And while capital punishment is controversial, it is realistically an issue that isn't so divisive as to cause an obvious rift. There remain plenty of no-go areas, where reform would be considered beyond papal jurisdiction, as they contradict historic teachings: the ordination of women, the acceptance of abortion, the recognition of same-sex partnerships as valid and pleasing to God.

Still, Francis has thrust the Church further to the left. But as the

Trump administration has proven, a disruptive conservative force has the ability to succeed a progressive legacy and dismantle it. Could this Pope's leftward moves be expunged by a more right-wing successor?

Here is where the inherent contradictions in Catholic teaching occur. The Pope is considered infallible, unable to speak in error, "when, in the exercise of his office as shepherd and teacher of all Christians, in virtue of his supreme apostolic authority, he defines a doctrine concerning faith or morals to be held by the whole Church." The doctrine was confirmed in 1870 at the First Ecumenical Council of the Vatican, but had been proposed for centuries. Problem is, it was also rejected for centuries by many senior Catholics, and there was a sizeable opposition to it in 1870. It's no coincidence that this was a time when the Church was under vehement attack in Germany and France, and liberalism was taking hold throughout the western world. It was, in effect, Rome reminding people who was boss.

But it also has limitations, in that it cannot be applied to what are considered new doctrines, but only to affirm what has been taught in the past. But what constitutes "new?" One could convincingly argue that Christ himself had women around him who were ordained, that he fully accepted gay people, and never spoke of abortion. Novelty, it seems, is in the eye of the beholder, and especially the beholder who enjoys ecclesiastical power. It's also unclear when papal infallibility is even being used, and there's disagreement about the number of times Popes have spoken thus — some say twice, others seven or even eight.

So the next best thing to an infallible statement is a line or two in the catechism, and that's what Francis has done. Further editing the catechism around this issue would be almost impossible for the next Pope; such a conservative, backward step would be devastating for the Church's international reputation. Short of an infallible statement, this is about as absolute as it gets.

In the past, Francis has spoken of the possibility of women deacons, of allowing divorced Catholics to re-marry in the Church, and made some positive noises about LGBT+ equality. But little has been achieved, and indeed on the last subject he's often dialled back the conversation; it is, for example, more difficult for a gay man to enter a Catholic seminary now than it was under the previous two Popes. On capital punishment, however, the leader of more than a billion Catholics has made an indelible impression on the world's stage, aligning his institution with the left of the political spectrum, and with the forces of progress and change. He's opened the door, knowing that within a few years when he is replaced, his successor as pontiff might not walk through it, but nor can he close it again. In a body as rigid, hierarchical, and torn as the Roman Catholic Church, that's an extraordinary achievement, and a holy legacy.

Maclean's, July 12, 2018

THERE REALLY IS no business like saint business. Once you make it, people pray to you, put statues of you in their rooms, and thank you when they recover from an illness — or just find a parking spot.

But the making of and praying to saints — and the entire hagiographical industry, for that matter — can be vulgar and achingly banal. It's not supposed to be that way, of course. At its best, it should represent a genuine desire to single out those who have sacrificed heroically, or have contributed magnificently to the betterment of humanity, for special praise. Alas, that purity was lost a long time ago.

It can also be political and acutely divisive, and that's certainly the case at the moment, as two prominent Roman Catholics of the early twentieth century move towards saint status: British author G.K. Chesterton, and Polish Cardinal August Hlond. Both men, especially the former, were accomplished and impressive, but they share a dark commonality too: they both made appallingly anti-Semitic comments in the 1930s, when the Jewish people were about to become victims of an attempted genocide. And the politics threaten to overshadow the whole process — not to mention the Church's well-intentioned and largely successful efforts to shake off its centuries-old reputation as an anti-Semitic institution.

Hlond, who died in 1948, was Primate of Poland and Archbishop of Warsaw, and is admired because he spoke out against both the Nazi and Soviet occupation of his country. He was also the only member of the College of Cardinals to have been taken into custody by the Gestapo. His canonization process began in 1992, and this May he was named as "Venerable" by Pope Francis. That's pretty advanced, and if a few miracles can be attributed to his intercession, he will be declared a saint.

Chesterton has further to go. His cause actually has its origins in Canada: Back in 1986, in a sermon at the end of a Chesterton conference at the University of Toronto, Cardinal Emmet Carter, the Archbishop of Toronto, argued with a wink that more laypeople should be canonized. I spoke at that conference and was present at the sermon, having written a biography of Chesterton, and it took until 2013 for the author's cause to be formally introduced; now his writings are being investigated with sainthood in mind.

The making of saints is complex, and on some levels absurd. It wasn't always that way, and in medieval Europe things were much simpler: A saint was proclaimed by popular demand. If enough people were sufficiently loud in the streets of Rome, you were in. Today, however, the panoply of the approved is distinctly odd, with violent, intolerant, and sexually neurotic types joined by authentically good and remarkable people.

In the cases of Chesterton and Hlond, both men had undeniable virtues as well as brutal flaws. Hlond was brave and defiant in standing up to the Nazis, but he also helped to empower their grotesque racism. In 1936, he wrote: "So long as Jews remain Jews, a Jewish problem exists and will continue to exist ... It is a fact that Jews are waging war against the Catholic church, that they are steeped in free-thinking, and constitute the vanguard of atheism, the Bolshevik movement, and revolutionary activity. It is a fact that Jews have a corruptive influence on morals and that their publishing houses are spreading pornography. It is true that Jews are perpetrating fraud, practicing usury, and dealing in prostitution. It is true that, from a religious and ethical point of view, Jewish youth are having a negative influence on the Catholic youth in our schools."

While he rejected violent attacks on Jewish people and property, he called for boycotts of Jewish stores. And while he condemned the Nazi treatment of the Jews, he refused to acknowledge the racist nature of Poland's post-war pogrom in Kielce in 1946, instead blaming it on what he claimed to be the Jewish support of communism.

Chesterton's issues are more nuanced. He died in 1936, before the Holocaust was fully operative or exposed, but had condemned Nazi anti-Semitism as early as 1934. But in alliance with his brother Cecil, a convinced hater of Jewish people, and the constantly angry author Hilaire Belloc, he was repeatedly and profoundly hurtful and harmful when it came to Jewish issues. This Roman Catholic triumvirate was renowned for an obsession with Jews, even at a time when casual anti-Semitism was far from uncommon.

The Brit wrote of a "Jewish problem," commented approvingly of the expulsion of the Jews from England in 1290, called on Jews in public office to be obliged to wear an identifying form of costume, and refused to believe that any Jew could be a true patriot. This led him to support Zionism and the establishment of a Jewish state in the Middle East. Then there were his ostensibly humorous poems that traded in troubling caricatures of Jewish people.

The consideration of the pair of candidates threatens to mask the modern reality that the Roman Catholic Church deserves enormous praise for its reformation of its relationship with the Jewish people. While long overdue, it should be acknowledged that since 1945, and in particular since the Second Vatican Council in the early 1960s, Rome has changed its language and approach, and demanded the same of its followers. Pope Francis is a loving friend of the Jewish people, John Paul II had an empathetic and intimate understanding of the Jewish experience, and the detritus of anti-Semitism is confined to the right-wing fringe of the Catholic world.

But that's why these two candidacies are so poorly timed. The Catholic right has re-emerged as a legitimate force in the Church in response to the more liberal Pope Francis, and Poland has just introduced extremely provocative legislation criminalizing discussion of any Polish involvement in the Holocaust. The timing could not be worse — and it's simply not worth hurting people or inflaming political situations for a political, curiously banal process.

Chesterton was a brilliant yet flawed author, and Cardinal Hlond a person of deeply questionable achievements. There are saints who have similar dark skeletons. But there is no need to open wounds or push these men toward something that is contrived and unnecessary. Better a sinner who clearly tried than a saint who clearly failed. Let's pray — to anyone we like — that it ends here.

Maclean's, November 27, 2017

ONE OF THE great myths about the Roman Catholic Church is that it is a single body, unified in faith and happily devout under direct guidance of the Holy Father — but that's hardly the reality.

While Catholic theology considers the Pope to be the direct successor of St. Peter, given the keys of the kingdom by Jesus Himself, the Church has always contained dissidents. And since the early 1960s, it has been acutely divided between conservatives and liberals — a rift that's grown deeper ever since the 2013 election of Pope Francis, the most reform-driven Pope in living memory and, after, the reigns of John Paul II and Benedict XVI, who were both adored by the Catholic right, the most polarizing.

With a decision on a particularly divisive papal text looming, there is a chance that 2018 causes the Catholic Church to come apart along those simmering seams. It won't be a formal separation — but it will certainly feel like one.

Critics of the Argentinian pontiff offer a litany of complaints: he is far too negative about Donald Trump; he embraces an abundance of progressive causes; during recent celebrations of the 500th anniversary of the Reformation, he's praised Martin Luther, who the right blame for splitting the Church in the past; and he promotes what they see as "pro-homosexual" priests in the Vatican. They argue that his desire to "make a mess," as he himself put it, means that he's indifferent to liturgy, and his commitment to climate change and his relative silence over issues of abortion and traditional marriage means he has betrayed his position. The more extreme even claim that he's lost legitimacy. The throne, they say, is empty.

The last holy straw could be coming in the form of a document entitled "*Amoris Laetitia,*" or "The Joy of Love," issued in April 2016 by the Vatican. This booklet seems to many outside of the Church to be absurdly esoteric, overwhelmingly obvious and even irrelevant. Within Catholicism, however, it is explosive. As with most Papal texts, it's long, dense, and open to various interpretations, but its most controversial element is that it allows Holy Communion to be given to couples who are divorced and have been remarried in a civil union.

Its meaning is layered in context, it is not rigid in its demands, and it calls for gentleness and for cases to be considered individually. But even so, it has sent countless traditional Catholics into paroxysms of rage. One group of scholars and priests sent an official appeal to petition the Pope to "repudiate" these "erroneous positions," and thousands of clergy have asked for "clarification" — the most severe criticism they can muster. That clarification is expected in 2018.

"Many faithful Catholics believe that with '*Amoris Laetitia,*' Pope Francis has encouraged beliefs and practices that are incompatible with the prior teachings of the Church," wrote Phil Lawler, the founder of *Catholic World News* — a conservative, but by no means the angriest of the righteous. "If that complaint is accurate, [Pope Francis] has violated the sacred trust that is given to him."

It's unlikely that Francis, now eighty-one and admitting to bouts with poor health, will retreat on "*Amoris Laetitia,*" and it may well be that he will open up even more discussion about the ordination of women as deacons — a position below that of priest, but exclusively male at the moment — and call for more dialogue with the LGBT+ community. We don't know all of the details but he has, for example, indicated that the all-important debate over married clergy may well be reopened. That will further provoke his critics, and many observers believe that to be one of the main reasons he will proceed. He may be the Pope, but he's a fighter and someone who doesn't suffer reactionaries lightly. He will want to open as many doors and windows as he can, before it's too late.

Some of Francis's critics have left the Church for Eastern Orthodoxy, and more still for one of the far-right Catholic splinter groups. One of his most high-profile opponents, American Cardinal Raymond Burke, has become more powerful and popular as the criticism builds.

But most are waiting to see what happens in 2018, especially those Catholic neocons in the United States and Canada who have spent decades in comfortable power in various journals, universities, and seminaries. The divide is ugly, and terribly lacking in Christian charity. Whatever happens, 2018 will be a year for Catholics living dangerously.

Maclean's, May 2, 2018

THE CONCEPT OF apology is at the heart of Christianity. It's right there in the Bible: "If we confess our sins, he is faithful and just and will forgive us our sins," says St. John. In other words, Christians may get things wrong — and may even commit terrible crimes — but acknowledgement of those errors, and genuine contrition, leads to forgiveness and a clean record.

Which makes it all the more galling that Pope Francis has continued to decline to formally apologize for his church's involvement in the grotesque treatment of Indigenous children in the residential school system. Such an apology was one of the ninety-four recommendations from the Truth and Reconciliation Commission, and the ask was repeated and requested by Prime Minister Justin Trudeau when he met with Pope Francis in March. He refused, and now Parliament has voted by a margin of 269-10 to formally invite the Pope to rethink his position. That's a polite way of insisting — and such an insistence from Ottawa is virtually unprecedented.

The decision has limited legal and constitutional weight, of course, but enormous emotional and political value. If Rome continues to withhold its apology, the optics will be severe. And even if it produces no results, it still exposes a church in crisis.

Up until now, Francis has said he takes the issue "seriously," but that "after carefully considering the request and extensive dialogue with the bishops of Canada, he felt that he could not personally respond." That's a pretty weak, and even dismissive response, but it's in keeping with the Catholic Church's approach; in 1991, the Canadian Bishops said, "We are sorry and deeply regret the pain, suffering and alienation that so many experienced" at the residential schools, and in 1993, they added that "various types of abuse experienced at some residential schools have moved us to a profound examination of conscience as a Church." It's all soaked in euphemism and clearly the product of legal vetting.

The essence of the Roman Catholic argument is that an individual diocese may apologize, but not the Vatican. The problem is that Roman Catholicism is centred on a supreme authority, and an apology from that authority is considered by Indigenous people to be essential. The Church, however, is terrified of the financial and legal repercussions.

Indeed, the Roman Catholic Church has also been asked to fulfil its financial obligations under the Indian Residential Schools Settlement Agreement, and to raise twenty-five million dollars for Indigenous healing, as demanded in the residential schools settlement of 2007. It has not come through.

The Church's Canadian champions are not helping. Sherwood Park-Fort Saskatchewan MP Garnett Genuis, for instance, said on Twitter that "Catholic entities involved in residential schools have apologized. The Holy See is responsible for next steps, & people are welcome to make their own judgments. It is not for Parliament to call out or dictate to one faith community." But this misses the point by a holy mile: None of the churches involved in the residential school catastrophe acted autonomously, and all of them were in partnership or in cooperation with the state. Parliament is not asking for the Catholic Church to apologize for what it did as a religious body, but what it did as a church acting partly as an organ of the state.

The government has already apologized, as have other churches. "We imposed our civilization as a condition of accepting the gospel. We tried to make you be like us and in so doing we helped to destroy the vision that made you what you were," said the Right Rev. Bob Smith in a United Church General Council statement in 1986. "We ask you to forgive us and to walk together with us in the Spirit of Christ so that our peoples may be blessed and God's creation healed."

And seven years later, Archbishop Michael Peers, Primate of the Anglican Church of Canada, issued a profoundly moving document: "I accept and I confess before God and you, our failures in the residential schools. We failed you. We failed ourselves. We failed God ... I am sorry, more than I can say, that we tried to remake you in our image, taking from you your language and the signs of your identity."

Now it's up to Pope Francis, for whom this represents another moment of truth as he swings once more between exuberant liberalism and strange stubbornness. Earlier this year in Chile, for example, he refused to apologize for the Church's history of abuse, and even criticized some of those who complained about what had happened to them. He later offered an apology, but only after an agonizing hiatus for the victims and a fierce reaction from the Chilean public. And while he has sometimes appeared as a compassionate reformer on LGBT+ issues, he's also given his blessing to a document that makes it impossible for even a celibate gay man to enter a seminary.

It's time for Pope Francis to make himself clear, once and for all, or risk the Church appearing to retreat back into the closed and frightened place it once occupied. There is much that is enlightened and compassionate about Catholic teaching, and it is those things — rather than its tendency toward being defensive and litigious — that need to be emphasized at this crucial juncture.

The Roman Catholic Church acted far too slowly, and sometimes callously, when the sexual abuse crisis was exposed. On residential schools, it has a clear choice, and it's one that it has to get right — for the Indigenous people of this country, but also for itself.

The Walrus, November 21, 2017

ALBERTA IS A divided province right now. The government is reforming its sex-education curriculum, and the province's Roman Catholic organizations are not happy. The Council of Catholic School Superintendents of Alberta delivered an alternative to the government's proposals, which it claims do not pay sufficient attention to religious sensibilities. Contrary to the government, the council states that same-sex relationships are "not part of God's natural order" and that gender identity is confirmed at birth. The province's Catholic school board is also demanding that it be allowed to apply Church teaching to questions around contraception, premarital sex, and homosexuality.

Premier Rachel Notley has rejected the proposal, standing by the status quo that the province's schools all teach the same curriculum. Newly minted United Conservative Party leader Jason Kenney, himself a conservative Roman Catholic — and quite possibly the victor of the next provincial election, in 2019 — supports the Catholic opposition.

None of this should come as any surprise. Back in 2010, then Ontario premier Dalton McGuinty backtracked on his own government's new sex-ed curriculum — the planned lessons were long overdue, and they emphasized that sex was pleasurable, that it consisted of more than intercourse, that spoke briefly of oral and anal sex, and that introduced the topics of homosexuality and gender fluidity. It was the sort of thing taught for almost twenty years in most of Europe and was supported by Ontario's public schools. Conservative Christians, backed by orthodox Muslims, however, thought somewhat differently. They didn't want homosexuality accepted, dismissed any concept of gender identification, were appalled at references to masturbation and non-penetrative sex, and — at heart — rejected the notion of anybody other than parents teaching children about sex. These parents, and various faith-based parent groups, exerted pressure on the government through media and protests. And it worked. It all just seemed too controversial for an already beleaguered government to handle.

It was an incredibly rare example of a reversal of policy, demonstrating the militancy and determination of those who oppose children being educated in a modern forum about sex and sexuality. Mind you, it must be said that after winning a Liberal majority in 2013, Premier Kathleen Wynne simply refused to bend to the hysteria and she reintroduced the curriculum. It's a decision, however, that has continued to dog her. The groups doing the dogging have money behind them and their puritanical bark is loud. On the evangelical side are people such as Charles McVety, president of Canada Christian College and someone who is also involved in a number of lobby groups. McVety is a frequent media guest, is well financed, and is linked to senior conservative figures in the United States. Another group is Parents as First Educators (PAFE), which has right-wing Catholic leadership, as does the anti-abortion Campaign Life Coalition, which is increasingly active on sex-ed issues.

The concerns of the critics of sex-ed in Alberta, Ontario, and elsewhere are many, but what drives their opposition is the certainty that knowledge will lead to activity. Opponents assume that if a child learns about sex in a classroom, they will be transformed into miniature fornicators and perfectly groomed victims for assorted predators and pedophiles. Only parents, they believe, can stop it from happening. Tory MP Brad Trost even compared sex-ed to the horrors of residential school. "We in Canada, when we have taken away those rights from parents, we have had a disaster each and every time. The most tragic incident in our history was the residential schools, and that was the underlying problem — parental rights were not respected."

In reality, sex-ed lessons are fairly clinical and even numbingly cold. As one sex-ed teacher told me, "Sexy this is not. Many of the kids are embarrassed, and a lot of them think it's funny or, the word I hear most, gross." If anything, these curricula are designed to reduce promiscuity and to teach young girls in particular that they have control over what they do and to whom they say yes. The idea of self-worth that permeates sex-ed. Dignity is a crucial element in sexual health and is what allows for mature relationships founded on consent. The same dignity applies to lessons about contraceptives — particularly if we are genuinely concerned with unwanted pregnancies and STIs.

The other growing fallacy is that the direct alternative to sex education in school is parental instruction. Tanya Granic Allen, president of PAFE, stated that Premier Wynne "does not get to tell us parents what our children will learn, we tell her what they will learn. Most parents don't want their kids indoctrinated by the state and whatever new fad is taking hold of society these days." In fact, the internet, rather than the home, is generally where young people find information about sex. Christian parents are hardly renowned for their willingness to broach these issues with their children, much less provide the straight talk needed. By sparing their kids an updated sexual education, and maybe even encouraging them to think sex is too lurid to be spoken about, parents risk shaming their kids into thinking the act is wrong.

Sex education is designed to remove that stigma and shame. Vancouver-based nurse Meg Hickling, who has worked in sex-ed for more than twenty-five years, told Global News "there are thousands of studies all over the world that show that the earlier you start, the healthier the children are going to be and the easier it is for them to make good, informed decisions for themselves." If children have the vocabulary, self-confidence, and educational tools, they are also more likely to understand what adult behaviour is acceptable and what is not — and feel more empowered to speak out about it.

It's hard to escape the irony that many of the loudest critics of sex-ed are conservative Roman Catholics, such as the members of Campaign Life and the Catholic Civil Rights League, whose Church was responsible for one of the most widespread abuse crises in modern history. This was not just about a minority of sexually corrupt priests violating children, but an entire system that denied and enabled and even took legal action against some victims. The very sex education that many conservative Catholics vehemently oppose is one of our best bets when it comes to reducing such systemic abuse — a curriculum that exposes abusive tactics can equip children to spot warning signs and navigate the euphemism and obfuscation on which abusers rely.

But the opposition doesn't even stop there. When I covered the two largest anti-sex-ed demonstrations at Ontario's Queen's Park in recent years, I noticed a monomania around the issue of homosexuality, or "sodomy," as opponents of sex-ed frequently describe it. There were numerous posters condemning LGBT+ teaching, frequent references to the Liberal premier's sexuality (she is openly gay), and plenty of talk of "Adam and Eve, not Adam and Steve." Risible as this may sound, conservative Christians seem certain that sex-ed is all part of a greater plot to make everybody gay. Lifesite, an extremely influential conservative Christian news website, stated that "[w]ithout regard for the religious/moral beliefs of families, the curriculum will normalize homosexual family structures and homosexual 'marriage' in the minds of 8-year-olds" and that "the Kathleen Wynne government will certainly take an activist approach to these lessons and show no respect nor tolerance for traditionally-principled families." It's not true, of course, but it's significant that the very thought of "normalization" of what is generally considered normal is regarded as abhorrent.

A few weeks ago, I wrote a satirical tweet about sex education: "I sympathize with those who fear that sex-ed will sexualize kids. Our youngest studied WWI on a Monday; by Friday he'd invaded Belgium." There were an extraordinary 230,000 "likes," but of the angry responses, I'd estimate that at least 20 percent alleged that sex-ed classes were grooming children to enjoy anal sex. That charge — now wide-spread in the anti-sex-ed industry — is based on a colossal lie. Protestors simply cherry-picked parts of curricula that mention anal sex. The truth is that the Ontario teaching program mentions anal sex only twice, in grade seven. The first reference stresses communication between partners and urges an informed choice about whether to delay sexual activity, including anal intercourse. The second is in the context of the risk of sexually transmitted illnesses. Nobody is instructed in the act; children are merely told that it occurs, that there are risks, and that young women in particular have the right to say no and to control their own bodies.

If anything can be learned from the Ontario example, it's that the protests are best ignored. In parts of Toronto, thousands of children — generally from Muslim families — were briefly withdrawn from school by concerned parents, but while this tactic seemed challenging at the time, it was soon abandoned and forgotten. There were also some cases of Christian families moving their children to private schools or turning to home-schooling, but the numbers were relatively insignificant.

Not all sex-ed critics are malicious. Sometimes, it's just generational naïveté and a form of overprotection. Such foot soldiers usually accept the changes in the curriculum when they realize that their children are just as they were, but perhaps a little happier and less intimidated. Good Lord, kids won't even do their math homework, let alone their sex-ed studies! Yet as one tweet to me had it, "We're not going anywhere and we won't give up. They come for the children first and we won't let it happen. Go to hell you perv." I did not retweet.

The Globe and Mail, August 15, 2018

AFTER TWO YEARS of research, a grand jury report based on what is likely the most comprehensive investigation in U.S. history into Roman Catholic Church child abuse has been released. Internal documents from six Catholic dioceses in Pennsylvania reveal that morethan "300 predator priests have been credibly accused" of sexually abusing more than 1,000 children. One victim was a girl of eighteen months, one underage girl was raped by a priest, who then arranged her abortion. A boy was made to stand naked in a crucifix position and the priest who photographed him then shared the images with other clergy on church property. One abuser, who left the Church after numerous abuse complaints, was given a reference by the diocese to work at Disney World.

In one case, a priest groomed children by telling them that the Virgin Mary had to "bite off the cord" and "lick" Jesus clean; another abused five young sisters from the same family and collected their urine, pubic hair and menstrual blood; one priest raped a girl who was in hospital after minor surgery.

The grand jury stated, "We believe that the real number of children whose records were lost or who were afraid ever to come forward is in the thousands. Priests were raping little boys and girls, and the men of God who were responsible for them not only did nothing; they hid it all. For decades. Monsignors, auxiliary bishops, bishops, archbishops, cardinals have mostly been protected; many, including some named in this report, have been promoted. Until that changes, we think it is too early to close the book on the Catholic Church sex scandal."

This comes after two weeks of international scandal involving the Church and abuse. Former Australian archbishop Philip Wilson was convicted of concealing child sex abuse and given a one-year sentence, to be served at home because of ill health. He is the most senior Catholic cleric to be convicted. Then Britain's Independent Inquiry into Child Sexual Abuse found that two of Britain's most prestigious private Catholic schools "prioritized monks and their own reputations over the protection of children" when over several decades children as young as seven were sexually abused.

Frankly, it will not be the last we discover of such horrors. The Church has reacted of course, but always slowly, usually reluctantly and often incorrectly. It still treats offenders leniently, still covers up when it thinks it can and still refuses to address the major causes of abuse. One horribly regrettable response, for example, has been to try to link sexual abuse with homosexuality. It's probably more difficult for a celibate gay man to enter a seminary under the allegedly progressive Pope Francis than it was under his more conservative predecessors. It's not only an odious fallacy, but also a painful digression.

In fact, there are three genuine issues. First is enforced celibacy. Men denied sex do not become abusers, but abusers do look for places where they can disguise their crimes. There are a large number of gay priests — estimates are between twenty-five percent and fifty percent — and these men, some in relationships and some not, have to live a lie. Abusers exploit this culture of obfuscation to hide their crimes. A solution would be to ordain married men and to allow gay clergy to be open and honest.

Second is the extraordinary patriarchy that exists within the Church. Women are not ordained, have very little influence and are excluded from decisions. While the presence of women doesn't make abuse impossible, it certainly reduces the likelihood. The vast majority of abusers in any situation are men; women are more often survivors and have greater empathy and sensitivity to the issue, and they inject a gender balance that makes an abusive context more difficult to maintain.

Third is the rigid sense of authority that permeates the Church, even under more liberal-minded pontiffs. This is still a clerical church, and until it is democratized, closed circles of secrecy will be formed whenever leadership is challenged.

The reality, however, is that the Church will almost certainly continue to regard loving same-sex relationships as sinful, will never ordain women, and as Roman Catholicism is based on absolute central authority, will not genuinely empower the laity.

Abuse exists everywhere there is a power imbalance, and the Church is not unique. But unless we admit that child sexual abuse within Roman Catholicism is due to systemic problems rather than human failing, the obscenity will not stop. Prayers simply aren't enough.

WHEN POPE FRANCIS became the leader of the Roman Catholic Church in 2013, he said he was going to "shake things up." Judging by what happened just a few days ago, he is a man of his word.

Speaking to Juan Carlos Cruz, a victim of clergy sexual abuse in Chile, the pontiff supposedly told him that God had made him gay, and that his sexuality "does not matter." Cruz spent three days with the Pope in the Vatican, and reported that Pope Francis explained of the man's homosexuality this way: "You know Juan Carlos, that does not matter. God made you like this. God loves you like this. The Pope loves you like this and you should love yourself and not worry about what people say."

If this is true, it is arguably the most revolutionary statement made by any senior Catholic priest, let alone a Pope, about this subject in modern history. Up to now the Vatican has only said that it doesn't comment on the Pope's private conversations, but has issued no clarifications or denials. That may still happen of course, and in the past various apologists have come forward to argue — often outrageously — that Pope Francis's comments have been mistranslated or misinterpreted. We will see.

While the self-evident belief that LGBT+ people are "born that way" may be standard thought among most people, it runs directly contrary to Catholic teaching. The Catholic Church spends an inordinate amount of time in its catechism discussing an issue that Jesus never even mentions, explaining that it sees, "homosexual acts as acts of grave depravity," that are "contrary to natural law," and that "homosexual acts are intrinsically disordered."

It attempts to differentiate between people being gay and having gay relationships, but this is grotesque, rather like comparing homosexuality to criminality — we love the sin, hate the sinner. What the Church has never done is to say that same-sex relationships are allowed, or that God made people gay. If He did, it means it was His plan, and thus has to be ordained and accepted.

Conservatives within the Catholic Church are apoplectic of course. Lifesite, a major supporter of Canadian conservative politicians, stated: "Pope Francis' alleged infelicitous counsel to a gay man, if not retracted, risks slowly killing the same-sex attracted by affirming them to death ... The souls of roughly two percent of the world's population are now precariously balanced on the tip of the cupola atop St. Peter's Basilica, waiting to see if the Church will save them through the telling of hard truths, or condemn them through affirmation. "

So where does this put Canada's two most prominent conservative politicians — federal Tory leader Andrew Scheer and Alberta United Conservative Party leader Jason Kenney — who are both devout Roman Catholics? Kenney is running his campaign strongly on parental choice, which is shorthand for supporting Catholic parents and schools opposed to GSAS (Gay Straight Alliances). It's going to be increasingly difficult to form a cogent position if GSA supporters can quote the Pope as their comrade!

Scheer has been less outspoken on the issue, although he only managed to become party leader with the votes of zealous social conservatives Brad Trost and Pierre Lemieux. It was Trost's campaign spokesman Mike Patton who said in a public video, "In case you haven't noticed, Brad's not entirely comfortable with the whole gay thing."

In Toronto, PC Party leadership candidate Tanya Granic Allen also enabled the new leadership, with most of her vote going to Doug Ford. He later dismissed her as a candidate for her intense social conservatism, but then invited right-wing Christian leader Charles McVety to be his personal guest at the first public leadership debate. McVety has been exposed repeatedly for his anti-gay remarks.

Ford probably doesn't care, or even know, about Papal opinion, but Kenney and Scheer certainly do, and so do various bishops and cardinals throughout Canada who routinely fight battles against sex-ed partly due to its references to homosexuality, and who support Catholic school boards that still make it almost impossible for teachers to mention if they're in same-sex relationships.

I doubt we will see very much progress and action on this issue for some time, but the door has been pushed open wider, and it looks as though it's impossible to shut it again. Canada is more than forty percent Roman Catholic, many of our political leaders are part of that church, and even progressive Catholics such as Justin Trudeau are accused of being inconsistent by some of their co-religionists. Perhaps, just perhaps, they will soon be able to ignore all of that nonsense. And that will be a good thing not only for Canada, but also for the Roman Catholic Church.

iPolitics, February 28, 2018

CANADIAN POLITICS IS proving to be fertile ground for the Roman Catholic right these days. There have always been leading Catholic politicians, but whether they were Conservative or Liberal, Trudeaus or Mulroneys, they were more on the progressive wing of the Church, and emphasized the separation of Catholic teaching from their own policies.

Not today. Andrew Scheer and Jason Kenney are committed, orthodox Catholics, and Ontario Progressive Conservative Party leadership candidate Tanya Granic Allen is the new heroine of traditionalist Catholicism. So it's an intriguing time for Cardinal Robert Sarah to be coming to town.

For conservative Catholics, Cardinal Sarah is an icon, seen as holding the line against what is seen in some circles as the liberalism of Pope Francis. In March, he will be delivering a public lecture at St. Michael's College at the University of Toronto, and leading a two-day retreat for the priests of the archdiocese.

The invitation is causing a great deal of dissent within St. Michael's, a college already divided due to alleged attempts made by president David Mulroney to restore St. Michael's Catholicity and move it to the right.

Beyond Cardinal Sarah's general theological and political conservatism, he's made several controversial comments about moral and social issues. Originally from Guinea, he was appointed Prefect of the Congregation for Divine Worship and the Discipline of the Sacraments in 2014. In October 2015, he said that the "idolatry of Western freedom and Islamic fundamentalism are almost like two apocalyptic beasts," and similar to Nazism and Communism. He wrote that, "we find ourselves between gender ideology and ISIS" — in Catholic parlance "gender ideology" is the movement to give full acceptance to the LGBT+ community.

He continued with the theme of juxtaposing western liberalism and gay rights, with Islamic fundamentalist violence and fascism. Islamic massacres and liberal demands, he wrote, "regularly contend for the front pages of the newspapers," referring to the terrorist attacks that had taken place in 2015, and juxtaposing these monstrosities with the U.S. Supreme Court decision allowing same-sex marriage. "From these two radicalizations arise the two major threats to the family: its subjectivist disintegration in the secularized West through quick and easy divorce, abortion, homosexual unions, euthanasia et cetera."

He also claimed that there were "several clues" revealing the "demonic origin" of the two movements, and that they were "violently intolerant, destroyers of families, society and the Church, and are openly Christianophobic." He continued, "We are not contending against creatures of flesh and blood ... We need to be inclusive and welcoming to all that is human; but what comes from the Enemy cannot and must not be assimilated," and "What Nazi-Fascism and Communism were in the 20th century, Western homosexual and abortion Ideologies and Islamic Fanaticism are today."

In recent months, he has modified his language a little. Of gay Catholics, he wrote patronizingly, "I came to learn how these poor souls suffered, sometimes because of circumstances beyond their control, and sometimes because of their own choices. I sensed the loneliness, pain, and unhappiness they endured as a result of pursuing a life contrary to the true identity of God's children."

Well, at least he didn't directly compare them to Nazis and the Prince of Darkness.

In his partial defence, to an extent he's only echoing the official teach-ing of the Catholic Church, which argues that homosexuality is an "objective disorder" and "ordered towards an intrinsic moral evil."

As jarring as this is, however, it is rare for Catholic leaders to use such ugly language. It also comes at a time when Catholic clergy and politicians are more sympathetic to the gay community.

In 2017, for example, prominent Jesuit Father James Martin published a book entitled *Building a Bridge: How the Catholic Church and the LGBT Community Can Enter into a Relationship of Respect, Compassion, and Sensitivity*. It doesn't address Catholic hypocrisy around the issue, the number of gay clergy — perhaps as high as a third, many but certainly not all of them celibate — or the archaic, even unbiblical nature of Catholic teaching on sex and sexuality, but it's a book that could not have been written under earlier Popes.

Last year Cardinal Müller, another conservative hero, came to Canada, where among others things he described Canada's moves towards a tightly controlled policy of assisted dying as "tragic." It's all rather embarrassing to many Canadian Catholics, but conservative Catholic politicians are uttering not a word of protest. It would be ... well ... a miracle if that ever changed.

Review, Reformation,
and the Rest

The Globe and Mail, November 10, 2017

Martin Luther: The Man Who Rediscovered God and Changed the World
by Eric Metaxas
All Things Made New: The Reformation and its Legacy
by Diarmaid MacCulloch
Heretics and Believers: A History of the English Reformation
by Peter Marshall
Martin Luther: Renegade and Prophet
by Lyndal Roper
Martin Luther: Rebel in an Age of Upheaval
by Heinz Schilling

GRAND ANNIVERSARIES ARE to authors and publishers what voters are to a politician. They love them, albeit briefly. We can wait all day for a biography of a specific character or a history of a precise event, and then they all come along at once. That's the case with the 500th anniversary of the Reformation, which is — all cynicism aside — a vital event in both the evolution and consciousness of Western society. On October 31, 1517, Martin Luther, a relatively obscure

Augustinian monk and academic in Germany, nailed the Ninety-five Theses to the doors of the Castle Church in Wittenberg, issuing a challenge to Rome, shattering the religious homogeneity of Europe and changing the world.

Changing the world is something to which Eric Metaxas refers in his book's title, but then rather spoils it with a reference to rediscovering God. That, in fact, is part of the problem with this entirely adequate, but tendentious life of Luther. History is best when we are convinced the players don't know the outcome, which of course they don't. That's not the case here. It's a "great life" explored rather than an intriguing story told. The author is something of a star in the American conservative Christian firmament, but the heaven in question is not quite as sparkling as all that. He has written biographies of Dietrich Bonhoeffer and William Wilberforce, so it was inevitable that a life of Luther would come along for the 500th.

In other words, he's a journeyman author and seems to write for the occasion rather than for the vocation. Not that this is a failed book, and the tale is told in generally accessible terms. A frighteningly devout young man who as a priest would tremble at the idea of celebrating the mass, Luther became increasingly uncomfortable with Rome's unethical behaviour and then its theology. He was as much a product of his opponents' reaction as his own ideas, but when obliged to search further into scripture and history found his Catholicism melting away and an alternative, "protesting" Christian ideal emerging from the resulting religious puddle.

Metaxas is reliable on Luther as an often-troubled man who had no idea what he had initiated. He is also delicate in writing of his marriage to the former nun Katharina von Bora and the death of their daughter, Magdalene, who died in Luther's arms. But the book is inconsistent, leaping from event to event with strangely unequal attention. It also often seems padded, artificially distended with information that any interested reader would find online or in any reference book. He lists, for example, all ninety-five theses and a full letter from Pope Leo X, who excommunicated Luther. The former, in particular, is obviously of central importance, but it interrupts the flow of the book and, as any biographer knows, there's none so tempting as an obliging original source that takes up a whole bunch of pages!

Oxford professor Lyndal Roper is a far superior companion for anybody who wants to encounter Luther for the first time — or, for that matter, who already knows the man rather well. In her intensely thorough, but always stylish biography, she places him firmly in his era but also as a figure of colossal historical significance. Luther's Disputation on the Power of Indulgences, as the Ninety-five Theses are also known, began an exponential process of theological and political revolution. It was a perfect political storm: the rise of nationalism, the development of printing, an increase in literacy and a festering resentment of Rome's power, corruption and arrogance.

Luther was a pioneer in the field, but far from the first to question the Catholic interpretation of Scripture and authority; that had been occurring for centuries. Popes and bishops seldom reacted well — the brilliant fourteenth-century English theologian and priest John Wycliffe escaped punishment thanks to powerful friends, but after his death his body was removed from consecrated ground and burned, the ashes thrown into the local river. Luther was not metaphorically taller than his reforming forerunners, but he could stand on their shoulders.

Then there was the almost manic energy, the combination of invincible self-confidence and a breathless determination to impose his will. Roper attributes some of this to Luther's childhood — she is compelling on the man's early days — and depicts how the more he was opposed and threatened, the more he felt called to rip apart the curtain of the religious status quo.

He was a figure of undoubted genius, but it's also likely he didn't entirely realize what he had done. He developed a new theology as he went along, one that would be known as Protestantism, then saw a fresh generation of dissidents take their places across Christendom. There could have been no Calvin, Zwingli or Cranmer without the plump German.

But if he often wrote and thought like an angel, he hated like a devil. This is something that both Roper and German historian Heinz Schilling show without any partisan reservation. Luther's infamous statements on the Peasants' War in the mid-1520s, for example, are chilling — particularly as the peasants in question assumed that Luther was on their side and felt encouraged by his work. He condemned them as "faithless, perjured, disobedient, rebellious, murderers, robbers, and blasphemers, whom even a heathen ruler has the right and authority to punish" and argued that "a rebel is not worth rational arguments, for he does not accept them. You have to answer people like that with a fist."

Worse because of its grotesque contemporary resonance was Luther's anti-Semitism. As both books explain, he began by being open and friendly toward the Jewish people, believing this attitude would lead to mass conversion. When it failed, he gradually turned against them and finally produced a long treatise entitled "On the Jews and Their Lies." In it he calls for the burning of synagogues and schools, the destruction of Jewish homes, the theft of Jewish holy books, forced manual labour and, if possible, complete ejection from the country. The Third Reich trumpeted this filth, as did many Lutherans. It must be stressed, however,that there were always valiant Lutheran voices — Bonhoeffer, murdered by the Nazis, being a great example — who disagreed, and since 1945 the Lutheran church has bared and beaten its soul over this issue and has been startlingly honest in its self-criticism.

Schilling puts it rather well when he writes, "This book is not about a Luther in whom we can find the spirit of our own time; this book is about ... a Luther whose thoughts and actions are out of kilter with the interests of later generations." That is an essential, robustly ethical prism. Roper's is the more satisfying of the two biographies, but read as partners — as daunting as that may be — there is little more to be said about the man.

The Reformation may have started in Germany, but it soon spread throughout northern Europe and beyond. France was far closer than we may think to becoming a pluralistic or even Protestant state at one point, and reform made major inroads almost everywhere outside of Spain and Italy. British academic and broadcaster Diarmaid MacCulloch was knighted in 2012 for his services to literature, and his writings have to a large extent shaped Reformation history. His genuinely masterful life of the archbishop and martyr Thomas Cranmer is one of the truly great modern biographies. This volume is a compilation of twenty-two essays tackling Europe as well as Britain and dipping with a delicious expertise into subjects as diverse as the Council of Trent, Tudor royal image making, the Anglican prayer book, and the alleged latitude of the Church of England.

MacCulloch also writes exquisitely. "If you study the sixteenth-century, you are inevitably present at something like the aftermath of a particularly disastrous car-crash. All around are half-demolished structures, debris, people figuring out how to make sense of lives that have suddenly been transformed." There, now pretend you're not hooked.

Peter Marshall has written a long overdue single-volume history of the Reformation in England, fifty years after the seminal work by the great A.G. Dickens. There have been numerous books about various aspects of what happened under Henry VIII and his three children — and many television accounts, from the sublime *Wolf Hall* to the ridiculous *The Tudors* — but no popular yet scholarly study as broad in scope as this one. It's become fashionable in historical circles to revise standard assumptions, making the case that Mary Tudor, known as Bloody Mary, wasn't really all that bad (she was) or that Elizabeth I was in fact intolerant and cruel (she wasn't), but Marshall is more responsible and thoughtful than that.

It's a profound book with a light touch — and all the more impressive in that the author is covering almost a century of intellectual, social and religious history. That demands a whole nest of intellectual disciplines and understandings, and while he's perhaps better on the early rather than the latter period, it will be a long time before the book is surpassed. And, of course, a long time before the next major anniversary.

As MacCulloch said in an earlier book, "So much of the story so far has not been about unbelief at all, but sincere and troubled belief. When the children of the Reformation and Counter-Reformation and the children of the Jewish diaspora turned on the religions that had bred them, they mostly sought not to abolish God but to see him in a clearer light." Let that light shine on.

Maclean's, October 25, 2017

IT'S PARTY TIME in the religious world. On October 31, Christians —
or, to be more precise, Protestant Christians, with a surprising amount
of support from the Vatican — celebrate the 500th anniversary of
the Reformation, when legend has it that German monk and professor
Martin Luther nailed his Ninety-five Theses on the door of the castle
church in Wittenberg, thus lighting the fuse that blew European
Christendom apart.

It matters far more than one might think, because it was not only
religion but politics, culture, and economics that would change in that
hammering's wake. In the document, Luther made public his condemnation of the sale of indulgences — money paid to reduce the time
spent in purgatory, a sort of waiting room before heaven, by relatives
and loves ones. But this academic disputation went further than that,
and it was a manifesto of criticism aimed at Roman Catholicism.
History, as it were, was given a reboot.

There is much that is positive about Luther. He liberated people
from rigid church control, gave impeccable energy to the idea of the
individual's relationship with God, and worked to eliminate corruption

and superstition. In many ways, he was a pioneer not just of religious change, but of modernity.

But behind his undeniable genius was a gritty nastiness. He could be crude, abusive, angry, and, perhaps most tragically, profoundly anti-Semitic — a legacy that needs to be grappled with, even 500 years later.

He started as a supporter of the Jewish people, arguing quite rightly that they had been badly treated by the Roman Catholic Church, and quite wrongly that they, if presented with what he regarded as a more authentic Christianity, would surely convert. In 1523 he wrote an essay, entitled "That Jesus Was Born a Jew," condemning the fact that the Church had "dealt with the Jews as if they were dogs rather than human beings; they have done little else than deride them and seize their property."

But the Jews did not convert, and Luther reacted appallingly. In 1543, he published "On the Jews and Their Lies," which today is shocking in its venom, and even for its time stood out as particularly cruel and intolerant. In the 65,000-word treatise, he calls for a litany of horrors, including the destruction of synagogues, Jewish schools and homes; for rabbis to be forbidden to preach; for the stripping of legal protection of Jews on highways; for the confiscation of their money. The Jews are, wrote Luther, a "base, whoring people, that is, no people of God, and their boast of lineage, circumcision, and law must be accounted as filth."

Some of his defenders have claimed that Luther was old and ill when he wrote this, ignoring the fact that he lived another three years after the essay and that most of us become mildly grumpy when we feel unwell, not genocidal. Plus, Luther had also managed to have the Jews expelled from Saxony and some German towns as early as 1537.

And regardless of his intentions, Luther's thinking on the Jewish people had a direct impact on history: the Nazis amplified Luther's anti-Semitism from the earliest days of the National Socialist movement.

It helped in the creation of the heavily Nazified and racist faction of *Deutsche Christen*, or German Christians, within the German Lutheran church, but perhaps more significantly, partly enabled the culture of anti-Semitism that made the Holocaust possible.

One especially repugnant case is that of Martin Sasse, the Bishop of the Evangelical Church of Thuringia during Kristallnacht in 1938. He feted the pogroms and the mass destruction of synagogues and Jewish businesses, and even tied it explicitly to Luther himself; just days after what was in effect the beginning of the organized slaughter of the Jews, he distributed a pamphlet entitled *Martin Luther on the Jews: Away with Them!* in which he claimed the Nazis were acting as Christians in their violent anti-Semitism, and that this was precisely what Luther would have wanted.

Yes, there was also a powerful anti-Nazi movement within Lutheranism, and the sacrifice and even martyrdom of those pastors and laypeople must never be forgotten. The Confessing Church, for example, was formed in opposition to the regime's attempt to unify all German Protestants into a single pro-Nazi church. Leaders like Martin Niemoller and Heinrich Gruber were sent to concentration camps, but survived; writer and activist Dietrich Bonhoeffer, who was accused of being part of a plot to assassinate Adolf Hitler, did not.

But Luther was not unique in his Christian anti-Semitism. It's such a grotesquely paradoxical reaction, of course; Jesus and most of the founders of Christianity were Jewish, but many of those claiming to love Him have hated His race and people. St. John Chrysostom, a major influence on the Eastern Orthodox Church, was virulently anti-Semitic; in 1555, Pope Paul IV issued a bull removing the rights of the Jews and subjecting them to communal humiliation. The examples are, alas, legion. Christians deliberately expunged the Jewishness of their faith and thus distorted it and shamed the teachings and life of that first-century Jewish preacher from Galilee. It's a birth defect of the historic church, and it didn't take very long for early Christian leaders to join the club — and while Luther did not codify his hatreds into tangible church policy, he left a heritage of antagonism and hostility all the same.

But 500 years later, have lessons been learned and wounds healed? Is the world a better and kinder place now because Christians have realized their colossal failures, stemming from one part of the Church's founding figures? It's a layered answer. The Roman Catholic Church formally rejected its doctrinal anti-Semitism at the Second Vatican Council in 1965, and Catholics have worked diligently and genuinely to build bridges with the Jewish world since then. And outside of fringe conservative movements within the Church, Rome has been largely successful. Protestantism is diverse by its very nature. Evangelical conservative Christians frequently adopt a Christian Zionist stance and are passionate supporters of Israel, even if often for mangled reasons; the underlying theology looks to the world's Jews moving to Israel en masse, thus hastening the second coming and the end times. Lots of fire and mayhem to come — sinners beware.

Liberal Protestantism, including most Lutherans, is less absolute. In 1994, the five-million-member Evangelical Lutheran Church in America spoke publicly of Luther's "anti-Judaic diatribes" and denounced "the violent recommendations of his later writings against the Jews." The Central Council of Jews in Germany had long asked for a formal statement from Lutherans on the subject of anti-Semitism, and just last year, the Lutheran Church in Germany obliged, condemning Luther's writings on the Jews and "the part played by the Reformation tradition in the painful history between Christians and Jews." The state Lutheran churches in Norway and the Netherlands have followed suit.

Other Lutheran churches reacted earlier; the American Lutheran Church, for instance, acknowledged it as early as 1974. In 1998, on the 60th anniversary of Kristallnacht, the Evangelical Lutheran Church in Bavaria issued a declaration that "it is imperative for the Lutheran Church, which knows itself to be indebted to the work and tradition of Martin Luther, to take seriously also his anti-Jewish utterances, to acknowledge their theological function, and to reflect on their consequences. It has to distance itself from anti-Judaism in Lutheran theology."

The situation is confused by the situation in the Middle East. Progressive churches have been some of the first to admit and condemn past anti-Semitism, but have been equally bold in criticizing Israel, sometimes stridently. Informed critiques of certain Israeli policies is certainly not the same as anti-Semitism, in spite of what some zealots might have us believe, but there are times when attacks on Israel by Lutherans, the United Church and other liberal Protestants do seem to lack historical context and sensitivity to the Jewish experience, and seem more angry at the Jewish state than committed to a greater social and international justice. There have, for example, been numerous motions and even decisions to boycott and disinvest from Israel while at the same time brutal Muslim theocracies have been largely ignored.

Put simply, one of the prime reasons for the creation of Israel in 1948 was because European Christians had acted against their faith and persecuted the Jewish people. It's imperative that Christians understand that, but it's unclear that enough of them do. But for all that, the twin solitudes of Jews and Christians were broken down long ago. William Temple, for example, became Archbishop of Canterbury in 1944 and helped co-found the Council of Christians and Jews; in 1943, he spoke out in the House of Lords about the Nazi persecution of the Jews, insisting that, "We at this moment have upon us a tremendous responsibility. We stand at the bar of history, of humanity and of God." That type of stance has been replicated and applauded myriad times since then and now, thank God, flows through the bloodstream of contemporary denominations. When in 2008 Lord Jonathan

Sacks, the chief rabbi of the Commonwealth, publicly referred to the Archbishop of Canterbury and the Archbishop of York as "beloved colleagues," he meant it. When in 1986 John Paul II entered Rome's Great Synagogue, the first Pope since St. Peter to enter a Jewish place of worship, the emotion was genuine.

As a Christian with three Jewish grandparents, I have hardly ever experienced any anti-Semitism in the Church. But as I celebrate this 500th anniversary, I will do so with reservations. Not because I regret the Reformation — far from it — but because the otherwise sparkling lens that Luther provided is not, for me and I know for many others, completely clear. And that's so terribly sad.

The Globe and Mail, September 15, 2017

WHEN THE U.S. Supreme Court finally legalized same-sex marriage in 2015, some anonymous wit said that they desperately hoped that the first couple to take advantage of the law would be named Adam and Steve. It was a response, of course, to the galloping homophobia of the Christian right and the fact that it constantly obsesses about what it believes was God's original design for and of humanity. Born again, alas, often means the same as being born yesterday. Thus the story of Adam and Eve has in many ways actually caused great harm and is still doing so.

To those who embrace the metaphorical nature of the tale — and indeed of much of the Hebrew Scriptures, the Old Testament — it's a story that is entirely unchallenging. The opposite of unquestioning religious belief needn't be doubt, but faith seeking understanding. Yet in a darkly nostalgic attempt to preserve a patriarchal certainty, some Christians have embraced a raw, unkind literalism. So there could be some good old book burning if they get their hands on this one.

What Harvard academic Stephen Greenblatt demonstrates in his new book, with a lyrical ease of narrative and a genuinely impressive breadth of scholarship, is that the Adam and Eve template is replicated in numerous other cultures and says relatively little that is exclusive to monotheism. He also looks to motive, origin, and source. When some of the exiled Jews returned to Jerusalem from Babylon, they were horrified at the destruction and decay. Ezra and his followers may be celebrated as champions of Judaism, but today we'd probably see them as fanatics who rejected the pragmatism and moderation of most of their co-religionists. Their response to Jerusalem's demise was to set about ethnically cleansing the city both physically and spiritually. They were also obliged to ask themselves how this could have happened to the chosen people, why so many defeats, so much pain? Simple. The first humans let the side down and punishment was inevitable. Adam and Eve, you've got some explaining to do.

None of this material is new and there is no absolute answer to when the first books of the Bible were written, but it's likely that propaganda was involved. Spin, an agenda or, God forbid, fake news! "Yet millions of people, including some of the subtlest and most brilliant minds that have ever existed, have accepted the Bible's narrative of Adam and Eve as the unvarnished truth," the author says. Whenever the Adam and Eve explanation of human origins came into being and whoever wrote it, it has mattered for 2,000 years and still does.

While the book is a history and an analysis of the Adam and Eve story, it is also an account of the author's wanderings and wonderings through the prism of the Scriptural account of the original founding father and mother. It's as though the first couple represent a rock thrown into the water and we are taken on a journey to follow the ripples. Greenblatt used the same vehicle in an earlier book about Shakespeare (*Will in the World*) and the results then and now are compelling. It's not a unique device, of course, but there's always the danger of it all becoming too solipsistic, too indulgent. Not here. We spend time with John Milton, a timeless poet, but also the dedicated spokesman of the revolutionary and regicidal Puritan regime of mid-seventeenth-century England. We read of St. Augustine, the early shaper of the Church whose influence on Christianity is incalculable, but not impeccable. We're told of Renaissance artist Albrecht Durer and his depictions, not only of Adam and Eve, but also of Christ and of those ordinary central Europeans whom he met and knew. And finally, there is Charles Darwin and his ripping apart of the seamless garment of faith and science. He may have caused hardliners a great deal of anguish but, even at the time, there were Christian leaders such as the author Charles Kingsley who were convinced that theories of evolution in no way undermined Christian belief as long as we took an intelligent approach to the creation story. Greenblatt then jumps from matters Darwinian to a delightful conclusion about his own time observing chimpanzees in Uganda.

He's strong and thorough on the misogyny that has been propagated by Eve's apparent weakness and manipulation and how it has drenched Jewish, Muslim, and Christian teaching. There's obviously a new theology at work today in certain circles, but it's difficult to expunge millennia of assumptions from institutions that rely on authority and hierarchy. Eve the temptress, Eve the mother, wife, pro-creator, helper, servant. Eve the object. Never Eve the leader or Eve the priest. It's often better than it was, it's seldom as good as it should be.

Greenblatt knows, as we all should, that ancient texts, whether they are religious or purely descriptive, always require interpretation. While taken in historical context and without banal anachronism the Old Testament is a vibrant, vital text — I certainly believe so as a Christian — but it's reductive and even dangerous to regard it as pure history. It was written and assembled at different times with different purposes, it's often tendentious and usually composed by the winners. As the author frequently tells us, the Adam and Eve morality tale is used to excuse and to justify at least as much as it is to illuminate and explore.

Perhaps more time could have been spent on the startlingly gender-free nature of much of Genesis in its original language and the fact that more than one account of the creation story is provided in the Bible, which is something religious zealots either do not know or choose to ignore, but that would be carping. This is iconoclasm with a delicate touch, never mean-spirited and intent on opening doors rather than pushing people through them.

By the way, that first married gay couple in the United States was not, unfortunately, named Adam and Steve. Oh well, we can't win them all.

THE 1962 MOVIE *The Last Days of Sodom and Gomorrah* is hardly the finest example of Bible epics. Stewart Granger tries his best as an Old Testament heartthrob, but the script groans and the plot bewilders. For all that, it's one of the very first lines that earns the film its place in bizarre cinematic history: "Watch out for Sodomite patrols!"

Watch out indeed. Christians have been watching out for a long time, causing incalculable pain, grief and suffering. Today, however, there is open debate within Christian and Jewish theology about the genuine teaching about homosexuality in the Hebrew Scriptures. Many of the most informed, erudite scholars are convinced that faith-based homophobia is a product of tendentious misunderstanding rather than historical and textual accuracy.

Which is where Michael Arditti's graceful and stylish work of fiction enters the fray. For more than two decades now, the British novelist and critic has been chronicling the influence of faith on our lives in a series of works that subtly sway believer and cynic alike. *Of Men and Angels*, to a large extent a collection of five novellas around a central theme, follows in that tradition.

In this case, that thread is the story of Sodom, where angels, commanded by God, destroyed the city with fire and brimstone. The elimination of Sodom and its neighbouring city Gomorrah is recorded, of course, in the Book of Genesis, and it's a story popularly known even in this Biblically indifferent age. It's why we have the word sodomy and why churches have traditionally supported the persecution of gay people — even now they often oppose LGBT+ rights and marriage equality.

Arditti takes issue with all of that, and with a delicate panache manages to weave modern scholarship into stories that range from the Babylonian exile of ancient Hebrews through a mystery play in medieval York in England, from Renaissance Florence and nineteenth-century Palestine to Los Angeles during the height of the AIDS crisis. He has angels framing the book, and occasionally whispering the narrative. "Yet just as I cannot but admire your ability to turn time-worn myths into a subtle and enduring theology, so I cannot but deplore the consequences," says the Archangel Gabriel. "And looking back at the earliest account of events in Sodom, I am amazed at the difference from the story that later became canonical."

Quite so. Thus we are introduced to Jared, one of the Jews taken to Babylon after Judah's military defeat. He is chosen to translate the Talmud, and realizes that the original account of Sodom is, in fact, largely lost. He becomes convinced that authentic Jewish values are irreconcilable with the hatred and destruction evinced in this part of Genesis. The Babylon where he lives is far more tolerant than he had been told, and his own sexuality is not condemned as it is in the revised version of Genesis.

And this is the key: Revisionism. What was considered absolute, immutable truth for centuries is now thought to have been edited so as to conform to a new puritanism and a need to distinguish the Jewish people from their powerful, and often seductive, conquerors. Simon

Muskham in fifteenth-century York participates in a local play about Sodom, but comes to see same-sex love as God-given and precious. Frank Archer, the final leading character, is a Hollywood star — echoes of Rock Hudson here — who, while dying with AIDS, begins his last, greatest movie, speaking truth to church power about the reality of Sodom.

It's all deeply moving and convincing, and one of Arditti's many strengths is that he doesn't allow the argument to dominate the humanity. He is convinced, and I agree with him, that the sin of Sodom concerns the rejection of the stranger, lack of hospitality, greed and mistrust of God. But he is disarmingly subtle in using this as a subtext, lived and breathed through his various characters. He is about story-telling and not propaganda; he is implicit rather than didactic.

On one level this is a novel of human failing and fragility, a splendid observation of our needs and desires, our triumphs and failings, told through the prism of history. On the other, however, it's a roaring indictment of the obsessive hostility toward homosexuality that even today flows through the bloodstream of the Church body like a toxin. It's the combination of these two literary brothers-in-arms that makes *Of Men and Angels* so compelling, and so vitally important.

CBC, March 10, 2017

AMERICAN EVANGELIST FRANKLIN Graham was in Vancouver last week, where tens of thousands of people heard the son of famed Rev. Billy explain how Jesus was the only way. Fair enough I suppose, but Graham's rather exclusive and harsh interpretation of the Christian message comes with a few strings attached: Islam is evil, Barack Obama is a friend of the Antichrist, Donald Trump is divinely destined, Vladimir Putin is a fine fellow and, naturally, gays and lesbians should be banned from churches because "Satan wants to devour your homes."

And now, Graham has identified and asked his legions of followers to help him oppose the new great enemy: the Disney movie *Beauty and the Beast*. I can hardly imagine that these sorts of people are Disney-viewers in the first place, but the premise for this concerted attack is fascinating, and it's already led to theatres banning the soon-to-be-released feature starring Emma Watson. Watson, mind you, came to fame as Hermione in the *Harry Potter* movies, which — according to fundamentalist Christians — was devil-inspired down to its wand.

As with so much that provokes the Christian right, it initially looks like this is a parody. How could a delightful movie about seeing authentic beauty in ostensible ugliness be un-Christian? How could a musical score that celebrates grace, dignity, female empowerment, and selfless love be offensive to God?

The answer is that the filmmakers remarked that there was a gay theme to the remake. In fact, it's less a theme than a blink, because if you look down at your popcorn for more than a moment you'll miss the bloody thing.

The most obvious change is that LeFou, the servant of bumptious swaggerer Gaston, is apparently gay. Director Bill Condon said it's a tribute to Howard Ashman, writer of the original film's lyrics, who died of complications from AIDS. Rather exquisite and touching one would have thought.

But if you're expecting LeFou — a figure of fun, remember — to protest about equal marriage or Russian homophobia, you're out of luck. His sexuality is vague and oblique to the extreme. The most obvious illustration is at the end when he dances with a male character who, as part of a comedy routine, is dressed in a woman's clothes. It's all about as sexual as a Don Cherry rant.

But the manic homophobia surrounding *Beauty and the Beast* is not a joke. It informs and infects what goes on within much of the Christian right in the U.S. and, to a lesser extent, in Canada: the opposition to so-called bathroom bills; teens being forced into conversion therapy; attempted and completed suicides; bullying and beatings. Because it also comes from Christians — albeit those on the ultra-conservative fringe — it also disgraces a faith that many of us hold to be sacred.

There's background and context here. The boycotters are the same people who urged people to see Mel Gibson's *The Passion*, even though it was absurdly sadistic and presented the suffering of Jesus in a manner that was humanly impossible. It was little more than Biblical *Braveheart*, with some of Mel's Jew-hatred and self-loathing thrown in.

There were also some on the Christian right who initiated a similar boycott against *The Lion, The Witch and the Wardrobe*, written by C.S. Lewis, arguably the greatest popular communicator of the Christian message in more than a century. Why? The title, silly. There's a witch in it, and the Bible is not overly enthusiastic about the species.

The movies that many right-wing Christians do enjoy are the *Left Behind* series, where the good people are suddenly assumed unto heaven and the rest of us, including children, stay behind in confusion. There are three films, and the scripts and acting are a lot like a Kellie Leitch video.

Then there is *God's Not Dead* and its sequel, where nasty liberals want to bully Christian kids and remove any reference to Jesus from the school system. These wretched things do well financially because they play into false fears and paranoia. And if you wonder where that sort of pathology leads, look no further than the election of Donald Trump.

One of the ironies here is that the hetero-hunk Gaston is played in the movie by openly gay Luke Evans, while his "gay" sidekick is portrayed by Josh Gad, who is as straight as they come. But that will escape the boycotters and the bigots, who prefer to perceive the world in banal caricatures. Problem is, those banal caricatures lead, in real life, not to harmless beauty but to dreadful and sometimes fatal beastliness.

CBC, December 25, 2017

BETHLEHEM HAS SELDOM been as calm as the Christmas cards make out, and 2,000 years ago the Romans and their collaborating friends in the Jewish population thought nothing of the occasional bit of slaughter. But was there a birth in, was it in winter? Were shepherds involved? And what has the modern Christmas got to do with it all?

To answer the last question: not much. There is a delightful new movie currently doing the rounds entitled *The Man Who Invented Christmas*, where Christopher Plummer as Ebenezer Scrooge and Dan Stevens as Charles Dickens show how the season of goodwill was moribund until *A Christmas Carol* appeared. Not quite.

The book was published in 1843, when Britain was being transformed from a rural to an urban society, with increased working hours, strain on families and wavering of traditions. Dickens wanted to emphasize the charitable nature of it all, to use it as a metaphor for social justice. The phrase "Merry Christmas" already existed, but Dickens was responsible for making it habitual, and the linking of Christmas with snow is also quintessentially Dickensian — perhaps the idea of a new purity, a washing away of dark, mid-Victorian inequality.

But Dickens was merely giving a reboot to a festival that had existed for centuries. Santa Claus or Father Christmas is a development of Saint Nicholas, a Greek bishop from the fourth century, possibly with a few hints of the Germanic god Wodan thrown in. The way he is depicted today is more Coca-Cola and Hollywood than the early church, but then most good stories are collections of earlier legends. Decorating trees, kissing under mistletoe, carol singing, puddings and the like have various origins — some ancient, others modern, all delightful.

Then we have the story that started it all — the one that it's so fashionable to be cynical about. The early Christians didn't celebrate Christmas, and Easter was the central event in the Church calendar. Actually, it still is.

In the fourth century, it was agreed to treat the birth of Christ as a holiday, but as scripture doesn't give any dates for the event — it had to be made up. Winter is doubtful because sheep herding takes place in the spring, but nevertheless Pope Julius I opted for December twenty-fifth, probably so as to appeal to pagan converts who observed the festival of Saturnalia in December.

There were other factors however. Many pre-Christian societies had long-established celebrations in December, and the winter solstice was important to northern Europeans who commemorated it with what they called the Yule, where logs would be put on the fire and those sitting around the flames would feast and drink.

It was also one of the few times when meat was readily available because animals were slaughtered due to the difficulty of feeding them in the winter. Add to all this the Roman elite's affection for Mithra, the god of the unconquerable sun, whose birthday was celebrated on December twenty-fifth, and we have a Christian holiday just waiting to happen.

But it's too glib, too convenient, to argue that the contrived nature of the Christmas holiday somehow means that there was no nativity and thus that the entire Christian story is — well — humbug. In my opinion, the only arguments as annoyingly facile as those of fundamentalist Christians are those of fundamentalist atheists. There is a middle way. The intelligent doubter will at least consider the ancient non-Christian writings that speak of the Galilean preacher whose followers called the Christ, and the intelligent Christian couldn't give a snow globe exactly when it happened, but that it did happen.

Belief in Jesus as the Messiah and acceptance of His teachings is something different of course, something more, than the acknowledgement that He lived. The former is an act of faith, the latter an act of logic. And faith has to be given voluntarily and never demanded. It's taken Christianity far too long to accept that fact alas, which is something to remember this secular, pluralistic Christmas. To quote Dickens' Tiny Tim, "God bless us, every one."

United Church Observer, June 2018

THE MAGICIAN'S NEPHEW by C.S. Lewis is being staged at the wonderful Shaw Festival in Niagara, Ontario, this season. It's the first book in the Narnia series, but was written after the far more famous *The Lion, the Witch, and the Wardrobe*. Countless children have read the seven Narnia books, just as legions of adults have read *Mere Christianity, The Screwtape Letters, The Abolition of Man, Miracles* and Lewis's other works. The movie *Shadowlands*, with Anthony Hopkins as Lewis, was a Hollywood triumph, three of the Narnia books have been turned into films and a fourth one, *The Silver Chair*, is expected late next year. In fact, the academic and author, who died in 1963, is arguably more popular and influential now than during his lifetime. But why?

Lewis's Christianity is beautifully argued, with a pristine logic and the crisp, consistent wit one would expect from one of the finest minds of the era. But there's also something about his image that many find appealing: the quintessential Oxford University professor, walking through the pub filled with pipe smoke, beer glasses, and tweedy friends, to proclaim the Gospel to an unbelieving world.

Still, it would be unfair to reject Lewis simply because of his popularity and because he is so beloved of those who like their Christianity certain and delivered in an English accent — indeed, Lewis was actually from Northern Ireland.

Walter Hooper was Lewis's friend and secretary in the last months of the great author's life. "He came to his faith via doubt, pain and even hostility," Hooper explained, as we sat in one of Lewis's favourite Oxford pubs. "In a way, it's a shame that some of his devotees think he offers easy answers. Far from it."

If Lewis demands anything of modern Christians, it's that we think and struggle with a faith that is never easy. When his wife, Joy Davidman, died in 1960, the man who told the world about belief lost his faith in a loving God. But only for a time. In the book *A Grief Observed*, he writes of this experience and of how "no one ever told me that grief felt so like fear."

Some of his writings appear a little dated to the modern reader, and his attitudes toward women at times groan in their clumsiness. But he also married a fiercely independent Jewish woman from New York, whose outspokenness was not always appreciated in postwar Oxford. It was because, not in spite, of that attitude that Lewis adored her.

Why is Lewis so popular today? Because he was clever, funny, empathetic, challenging, compelling, and invincibly Christian. "I believe in Christianity as I believe that the Sun has risen, not only because I see it, but because by it I see everything else," he wrote. Another gem: "Christianity, if false, is of no importance, and if true, of infinite importance. The only thing it cannot be is moderately important."

The persona is attractive to some, but the writings should be crucial to all. Lewis himself never thought he would leave much of a legacy. On that he was profoundly wrong.

The Walrus, April 2019

LAST MARCH, A story broke that must have had the sinners of the world praising whatever god they did or didn't believe in: Pope Francis, leader of more than a billion Roman Catholics, had apparently declared that hell didn't exist. Atheist journalist Eugenio Scalfari, cofounder and former editor of the Italian newspaper *La Repubblica*, reported that after a private interview, Francis had said that while the souls of repentant sinners "receive the forgiveness of God ... the souls of those who are unrepentant, and thus cannot be forgiven, disappear." In other words, it's game over for those sinners, which is a little depressing, but at least they can expect no post-death punishment. As happens so often with this outspoken pope, however, the Vatican's communication team quickly stepped in and denied that Francis made the statement at all. It was not the first time that the idea of hell has been questioned by an influential Christian. Rob Bell, a former evangelical church leader, argued a similar point in his bestselling 2011 book, *Love Wins*: "Has God created millions of people over tens of thousands of years who are going to spend eternity in anguish?" he asks. "Can God do this, or even allow this, and still claim to be a loving

God?" Clearly, the ancient idea, and veracity, of eternal damnation is still up for debate. According to a 2014 survey by the Pew Research Center, only fifty-eight percent of Americans believe in hell, though seventy-two percent believe in heaven. Almost all major religions, monotheistic or otherwise, have featured some hierarchy of reward and penalty after death. The specifics are debated — some faiths describe endless torture, others a place for introspection — but the concept of consequences in the afterlife has been a constant. Is our waning attachment to hell, then, a momentary blip, or are believers finally ready for faith that isn't tied to fear of everlasting agony? As Nova Scotia-based journalist and author Marq de Villiers explores in his new book, *Hell and Damnation: A Sinner's Guide to Eternal Torment*, our ideas around what happens after death have always been in flux. De Villiers' text is a deliciously cynical analysis of the afterlife viewed from a variety of historical and literary perspectives. He opens with a simple query, "What is this thing called hell?" Though, like any question wrapped up in thousands of years of religious interpretation, it depends whom you ask.

Hell has had many rulers. De Villiers refers to the "Big Men such as Hades, Tartarus, Beelzebub ... and the occasional Big Woman" who have been tasked with deciding the unfortunates on the underworld's guest list. In Christianity, it's Satan (derived from ha-Satan or "the adversary" in Hebrew) a favoured angel who, after some conflict with God, was kicked out of heaven. He then divided time between hell and Earth, where he has caused all sorts of trouble for us humans. Though some Christians claim their faith is immutable, many of its interpretations have indeed changed — Satan and hell being good examples. De Villiers argues, mischievously, but not entirely unfairly, that Old Nick has gotten a bad rap over the centuries: Satan was originally seen as a more neutral figure within the Church, one who reflected the darker side of human nature that must be struggled against.

During the Middle Ages, de Villiers writes, "Satan more and more took on his sinister shape as chief villain and chief prisoner, locked away by God yet with the ability to indulge in unlimited malice." This change came about partly due to the rise of dissent within the Church. After the Protestant Reformation occurred, in the sixteenth century, certain leaders in the Roman Catholic Church sought to link criticism of leadership with evil. The papacy emphasized the fires and torments of hell for sinners — including heretics — partly because the new Protestant alternative to Rome looked increasingly compelling. Another theory on why the idea of hell became so prominent suggests that much of Europe's ruling class — and the Church with which they sometimes enjoyed a symbiotic relationship — was terrified that the fear of earthly punishment was insufficient to assure order. But this thesis assumes that the certainty of hell produces good behaviour, and that clearly wasn't the case — the devil and his instruments, after all, were readily accepted at a time when massacres and murders were common. Other religions have been less concrete in their approach to damnation. For Buddhists, the closest word for hell would be Naraka — a place where some beings go because of poor actions taken in life. "Buddhists were often indefatigable travellers," writes de Villiers. "And many of them visited the infernal regions, sometimes out of sheer curiosity, sometimes out of piety, and sometimes apparently just for the hell of it." Naraka, however, is never said to be eternal, and its residents are free to leave after a few hundred million years. Meanwhile, Islamic texts describe a place called Jahannam, where sinners will be punished physically as well as spiritually. There is a lot of fire in Jahannam — indeed, in many religions, flames are linked to ideas of purging and cleaning, as well as being bloody painful. Judaism is the least punitive and precise of the Abrahamic faiths on the issue of hell. Jewish texts instead speak of Gehinnom, which is more like a purgatory — a place where the dead are judged according to their earthly actions and made aware of their failings. Interestingly enough, most adherents to Judaism didn't even imagine a retributive afterlife until they were exposed to Hellenic ideas around 400 BCE. Ancient Greek thought was multi-faceted, but the mythology envisaged a gloomy place below the underworld of Hades called Tartarus, where torture and suffering were meted out to a deserving few. When Jews became steeped in Greek culture, they picked up some of these beliefs around retribution, and as the diaspora travelled, its theology was influenced accordingly. Not all religious leaders spent time thinking of the many ways people could and should be punished. De Villiers writes that some African and Australian cultures were rare in not having any specific language for hell or any concepts of post-death judgment either. "There was really no need," de Villiers writes. "Sure, the world has a creator, who had to live somewhere, often in what seems rather like a summer resort for himself, his family, and various magical minions, but this had little to do with ordinary people." In these cultures, there was no "clear dividing line between life and death; these were not mutually exclusive." What many would consider death was, for them, simply a change, not a finality.

Not long ago, Christians — especially Roman Catholics — were convinced that suicide led to hell. Now that belief is often rejected. This may be partly because people have, generally speaking, become more empathetic, and there is an increased comprehension of the realities of mental illness. As we understand more of the world, our beliefs tend to change — hell, therefore, is partly a product of us. We see that in the way secular society has dragged more progressive churches — and the Catholic reality if not the ideology — away from conversations about eternal punishment and toward those about the need for voluntary goodness, which, I'd argue, is far more synchronized with the original teachings of Christ. It's not that people no longer believe in the difference between right and wrong; rather, hell may have fallen out of favour precisely because people believe in making decisions out of love rather than legalism. And that, if you think about it, is rather heavenly. "The systems we create are therefore our systems, not his," de Villiers writes, referring to God. "They are infinitely malleable, and require constant vigilance, frequent updating, and unending skepticism from an engaged citizenry." But I am, for my sins, a Christian, and I believe that faith is a dialogue. I take a literary and critical view of scripture and appreciate its metaphors and poetry as well as its truth and virtues. Most of the best people I know are atheists and agnostics, and I believe that Christianity is regularly shamed and stained by its hell-believing adherents. I've spent the last three years studying for a Master's of Divinity, and while I now know more about hell than ever before, I understand it less than ever. Perhaps that's the way it's supposed to be. In a list of hellish possibilities, de Villiers writes of "cauldrons of boiling oil," a place "full of stench and noise and pain, torment its sole purpose," and "ever-burning wrath." He ends, however, with something different: "Hell is just a state of mind, a radical separation from god." This idea I like. If God is love — and why otherwise would we bother? — surely the worst thing imaginable is to be cut off for all time from authentic, meaningful, selfless love. As to what that love is and how we find it, I'll be damned if I can give any satisfying answers.

The Globe and Mail, July 15, 2019

THREE YEARS AGO I wrote with joy and pride that the Anglican Church of Canada had voted at its Synod (the church's governing body) to approve equal marriage, to give formal and sacramental acknowledgment of the church to LGBTQ people who wanted to embrace holy and lifelong commitments. In other words, gay men and women could be married in Anglican churches.

The vote was extremely close, and a two-thirds majority is required in the three orders of laity, clergy and bishops. Still, it succeeded. A second approval was required, however, and in Vancouver on Friday that didn't happen. While the clergy and laity overwhelmingly approved, the order of bishops gave only 62.2 percent support, just one or two votes shy of what was required.

People reacted with shock, because even though the church did pronounce that each diocese could move ahead as it sees fit — several have already married same-sex couples and will continue to do so — this was a body blow, especially to those gay Christians who have remained faithful worshippers in spite of rejection.

The Bishop of Niagara, Susan Bell, spoke for many when she said,

"My heart aches with lament and my soul is filled with anguish know-ing all the pain and hurt caused by the General Synod's failure to ratify a change to the national marriage canon that would have explicitly expanded the meaning of marriage to include same-sex couples."

Yet she continued, "The General Synod did also overwhelmingly vote to affirm the prayerful integrity of the diverse understandings and teachings about marriage in the Anglican Church of Canada ... As a result, nothing about this decision will change our practice in Niagara. I remain steadfast in exercising my episcopal prerogative to authorize the marriage of all persons who are duly qualified by civil law to be married, thereby responding to the pastoral needs present within our diocese."

So, while this is enormously hurtful and damages the church's reputation in the public square and in particular among younger people, it is by no means the final statement. Also, for a church to live authentically, it has to listen to all voices, even if they may appear jarring. But why the continued opposition to what is essentially a call for unconditional love?

The subject is hardly mentioned in the Bible, and when conser-vatives quote the Old Testament they often do so without a thorough understanding of its nature. The Hebrew Scriptures aren't linear history and certainly don't constitute a handbook of modern life — they sometimes defend slavery, demean women, even advocate ethnic cleansing. They're to be understood through context and reason. For example, the story of Sodom and Gomorrah, the sinful cities destroyed because of their wickedness, is far more concerned with respecting guests than condemning gay people — the homophobic interpretation arrived centuries later.

When the Old Testament does mention homosexuality, it also forbids the combinations of certain cloths, eating the wrong foods, or inter-course with a woman when she is menstruating. I have no recollection of any of these subjects being debated at a church synod.

Jesus never mentions homosexuality, and stands in sparkling contrast to many of his contemporaries in being largely indifferent to people's private sex lives. The song of the Gospels is justice, hope, compassion, and love; it sings of inclusion and grace and tolerance.

There may, however, be one story in the New Testament where Christ does respond to a same-sex relationship. It's where a Roman centurion asks for his slave, a man he has come to love, to be cured. This soldier is the personification of the occupation, a gentile and an oppressor, hated by the Jewish people. More than this, the Roman military were often mocked by the Jews as men who returned to their barracks to engage in sex. This Roman also uses a specific Greek word to describe his relationship with his servant that goes beyond the platonic. Yet Jesus is in awe of the man's faith, and heals with praise rather than condemnation.

St. Paul does indeed write, albeit briefly, about what we might today call homosexuality, but his disapproval is for heterosexual men using boys for exploitative sex, not for loving partnerships. Paul is responding to pagan rituals that used homosexual rape as a form of initiation, and while his genius is beyond doubt, he says nothing about equal marriage that has any relevance to the modern conversation.

It's not over, and the disagreements will, alas, continue. But so many of us, gay and straight, so wish we could just listen to Jesus, welcome equal marriage, and then simply move on. Please God.

We acknowledge the sacred land on which Cormorant Books operates. It has been a site of human activity for 15,000 years. This land is the territory of the Huron-Wendat and Petun First Nations, the Seneca, and most recently, the Mississaugas of the Credit River. The territory was the subject of the Dish With One Spoon Wampum Belt Covenant, an agreement between the Iroquois Confederacy and Confederacy of the Ojibway and allied nations to peaceably share and steward the resources around the Great Lakes. Today, the meeting place of Toronto is still home to many Indigenous people from across Turtle Island. We are grateful to have the opportunity to work in the community, on this territory.

We are also mindful of broken covenants and the need to strive to make right with all our relations.